INDONESIAN

John B. Kwee

TEACH YOURSELF BOOKS
Hodder and Stoughton

First printed 1965
Second edition 1976
Twelfth impression 1991

Copyright © 1965
Hodder and Stoughton

ISBN 0 340 20380 3

Printed in Great Britain
for Hodder and Stoughton Educational,
a division of Hodder and Stoughton Ltd,
Mill Road, Dunton Green, Sevenoaks, Kent
by Clays Ltd, St Ives plc

CONTENTS

PREFACE

Though the members of the 200 Indonesian ethnic groups speak their respective vernaculars among themselves, they also speak and understand Indonesian.

A foreigner with some knowledge of Indonesian might travel to the remotest area or set foot on the smallest island of Indonesia, and yet meet someone from whom he could ask information.

Though the native's Indonesian might be as poor as the foreigner's they could make themselves understood. A short sentence, even a word could rescue one from difficulty.

—**Di mana rumah tukang-pahat?**	—Where does the sculptor live?
—**Di situ**	—Over there
—**Jauh?**	—Is it a long way off?
—**Tidak, dekat saja**	—No, it's near by
—**Mau antar saya?**	—Would you show me the way?
—**Baik**	—All right

The conversation above is simple, yet clear and straightforward. The author is convinced that by regular use of this book the student will be able, in a fairly short time, to make better and longer conversations than the example above and read not too difficult Indonesian books.

The exercises at the end of the chapters are so varied as to give the student an opportunity to think in Indonesian while making up the answers.

The key at the end of the book should be consulted only after the exercises have been done.

This book finishes with a vocabulary of Indonesian–English and English–Indonesian words and some important Indonesian derivatives.

The author wishes the student of this book 'SELAMAT BELA-JAR'.

INTRODUCTION

Indonesian is a fairly new language. It has developed from Malay, which in the fifteenth century was the *lingua franca* of the prosperous kingdoms of the Malayan peninsula and the coastal harbour towns of the Indonesian archipelago.

Arab merchants brought much influence to Malay, and the Malayan script, based on the Arabic script came into existence.

In the seventeenth century, Portuguese and Dutch traders set foot in Indonesia, and Malay became the language of commerce between the Europeans and the Indonesian spice merchants.

During the Dutch rule, Dutch authorities used Malay to make contact with the Indonesian sultans and chieftains.

In 1918 Indonesian members of 'Volksraad' (Parliament) moved a motion, proposing that Malay should be used at the Parliament sessions. This was granted by the Dutch.

Indonesian men of letters and journalists did their utmost to popularize Malay.

Balai Pustaka, a publishing house and library, was established and a great number of books and magazines was issued. Thus the Indonesian literature was born.

At the youth conference, which was held in Jakarta in 1928, Indonesian youth pledged that 'we speak one language: the Indonesian language'.

Efforts were made to abolish 'Melayu Pasar', a jargon which was widely spoken, and replace it with modern Malay.

A conference on the forming of the Indonesian language was held in Solo (Central Java) in 1938. A historic resolution was passed: modern Malay was to be the basis of the Indonesian language.

In 1949 the Indonesian government officially declared that the Republic of Indonesia had one national language: the Indonesian language.

Today, Indonesian is spoken by over 150 million people living in the Republic of Indonesia, which consists of approximately 3000 islands, covering an area as large as the continent of Europe. Over 200 ethnic groups, each with a vernacular of its own, inhabit the island republic.

I Script
II Pronunciation and Spelling
III Accent

I Script

Indonesian used to be written in a script adapted from Arabic. Nowadays Roman letters are used.

The Indonesian single vowel symbols are: a, e, i, o, u.

There are only three double vowel symbols: ai, au, oi.

The single consonant symbols are: b, c, f, g, h, j, k, l, m, n, p, r, s, t, w, y, z.

The double consonant symbols are: kh, ng, ny, sy.

The consonant symbols q, v, x, occur very rarely.

II Pronunciation and Spelling

Indonesian letters represent one sound each. In other words, the letter *o*, for example, does not represent as many sounds as the English *o* does. One who studies English must decide whether to pronounce ou [ʌ] as in rough; [ɔ] as in cough; [u:] as in through; [ou] as in mould; [ə:] as in journey; [ɑuə] as in hour or [ɔ:] as in pour.

This difficulty will not be encountered by students of Indonesian. Except for a few letters, the Indonesian letters represent one sound each.

Vowels

a sounds like English *a* in 'far' but is slightly shorter and is pronounced more open and further forward in the mouth. In closed syllables it is pronounced slightly shorter than in open syllables.

kamar	room
apa	what
mahal	expensive

e when unstressed sounds like English *a* in 'among'; when stressed it sounds like English *e* in 'let'.

kera	monkey	**mentéga**	butter
mentah	unripe	**mérah**	red
semak	bush	**pésta**	feast

As Indonesian does not have an accent mark, it is rather difficult for the student to differentiate **e** from **é**. In good Indonesian dictionaries, however, **é** is accented. For the sake of clarity in pronunciation the **é**'s in this book will be accented.

i in open syllables sounds like English *ee* in 'seen' but is rather shorter, in closed syllables it sounds exactly like English *i* in 'tin'.

iri	jealous	**pasir**	sand
ikut	join	**asin**	salty
kipas	fan	**cincin**	ring

o sounds like English *o* in 'hob'

obor	torch	**kotor**	dirty
obat	medicine	**potong**	cut

Note: **o** in the following words is pronounced as the Italian *o* in 'O Sole Mio'. It is a single rounded vowel sound.

oto	motor-car	**soto**	a kind of soup
toko	shop	**radio**	wireless
mobil	motor-car	**foto**	photo
dosin	dozen	**téori**	theory
sosial	social	**perangko**	stamp
polisi	police	**pidato**	speech
produksi	production	**dinamo**	dynamo
résiko	risk	**loteré**	lottery
koloni	colony	**nasional**	national

u sounds like English *u* in 'put' but is slightly longer.
muka, face; **buku,** book; **itu,** that

Note: The letters **aa** which occur in a few words are pronounced with a slight hiatus between them, e.g. **saat** (pronounced *sa'at*), moment; **maaf,** excuse; **manfaat,** gain.

Diphthongs

ai in open syllables sounds like English *i* in 'like'; in closed syllables it is pronounced with a slight hiatus between **a** and **i**.

ramai	bustling, noisy	**kain**	(pronounced *ka'in*)	cloth
badai	storm	**kait**		hook
pantai	beach	**main**		play

au in open syllables sounds like English *ow* in 'cow'; in closed syllables it is pronounced with a slight hiatus between **a** and **u**.

pisau	knife	**daun**	(pronounced *da'un*)	leaf
danau	lake	**haus**		thirsty
harimau	tiger	**kaus**		socks

EXCEPTIONS: **mau,** will, shall, want; **bau,** smell, though open syllables, are pronounced with a hiatus between **a** and **u**.

oi represents the same sound of English *oy* in 'boy'. There are only three words with this sound viz., **sepoi-sepoi,** breezy; **amboi!** interjection, used to express surprise, pity, etc. (English 'alas!'); **Kroi,** a proper name.

Note: 1. The diphthong **ai** should not be confused with **a** followed by the suffix -**i.** The latter is always pronounced with a hiatus between **a** and **i.**
Compare: **ramai** and **melukai** (pronounced *meluka'i*), to wound, from **luka,** wound.

2. The letters **ia, ua, iu** and **ui** are not diphthongs. They are pronounced with a glide between the first and second element, e.g. **ia,** he, she; **dua,** two; **siul,** whistle; **peluit,** siren.

Consonants

b at the beginning of a syllable is pronounced like English *b* in 'bad'.

babi, pig; **abu,** ash; **badan,** body

when **b** is a final letter, it is pronounced like English *p*

bab, chapter; **sebab,** because; **nasib,** fate

c is pronounced almost like English *ch* in 'chair' but with the tip of the tongue further forward just above the teeth. The word **cét** (paint) is pronounced as if it were *t+yet*. Try to pronounce it without pushing the lips forward.

cacing, worm; **cincin,** ring; **cucu,** grandchild

d at the beginning of the word is pronounced like English *d* in 'day'

dari, from; **dan,** and; **dasi,** tie

When **d** is a final letter it is pronounced like English *t*.

abad, century; **abjad,** alphabet; **nékad,** reckless

f represents the same sound as the English *f* in 'far'.

fajar, sunrise; **faktor,** factor; **fantasi,** fantasy

Very often **f** is replaced by **p,** e.g. **fikir →pikir,** think; **fasal →pasal,** paragraph; **famili →pamili,** family.

g is pronounced like English *g* in 'go'.

garam, salt; **gigi,** tooth; **gula,** sugar

h at the beginning of the word and between two identical vowels is pronounced like English *h* in 'hat'.

hari, day; **pohon,** tree; **dahan,** branch

When **h** stands between two different vowels it is not pronounced.

lihat (pronounced *liat*), see; **tahu,** know; **pahit,** bitter

EXCEPTIONS: **Tuhan,** God; **mahir,** skilled; **lahir,** born; **pihak,** side; **rohani,** mental; **rahib,** hermit; **johar,** name of a tree. Here **h** is pronounced, though it stands between two different vowels.

When **h** is a final letter it is pronounced softly.
 buruh, labour; **tujuh,** seven; **roboh,** collapse

j is pronounced like English *g* in 'gentleman'.
 janji, promise; **judi,** gamble; **ijin,** permission

k at the beginning of a syllable sounds like English *k* in 'king', but it is pronounced without an 'explosion'.
 kaki, leg; **kuda,** horse; **kopi,** coffee
When **k** is a final letter it is not 'exploded' as it is in English. The word **masak** (to cook) leaves the speaker with an open mouth but without an 'explosion' of sound. It is cut off short with a jerk like the *o* of 'got' is jerked when 'I got it' is pronounced in an illiterate way.
 hak, right, claim; **dakwa,** accuse; **takluk,** surrender

kh sounds like the German *ch* in 'ich' and the Scottish *ch* in 'loch'. Words with **kh** are mostly of Arabic origin.
 khas, typical; **khusus,** specific, **khayal,** imagination

l is always pronounced like the initial English *l* in 'loose'.
 lupa, forget; **bola,** ball; **kapal,** ship

n represents the same sound as the English *n* in 'no'.
 nomor, number; **péna,** pen; **Senin,** Monday

Note: **ngg** represents the sound of **ng** in 'longer', e.g. **hingga,** until; **bangga,** proud; **tinggal,** live, stay.

ny sounds like English *n* in 'new'; however, it must be pronounced as one sound.
 nyala, flame; **nyanyi,** sing; **nyonya,** madam

m is pronounced like English *m* in 'man'.
 makan, eat; **Kamis,** Thursday; **alam,** nature

p sounds like English *p* in 'pen', however, it is pronounced without an 'explosion'.
 asap, smoke; **pipa,** pipe; **sopir,** driver

r   is trilled like Italian *r*.
       rusak, out of order; **bakar,** burn; **iris,** slice

s   represents the same sound as *ss* in 'boss'
       baris, row; **susu,** milk; **tas,** bag

sy   is pronounced like English *s* in 'suit' (sju:t).
       syak, doubt; **syarat,** condition; **syukur!,** thank God!

t   sounds like English *t* in 'tin', however, it is pronounced without an 'explosion'.
       tampar, rope; **tutup,** close; **mayat,** corpse

w   sounds like English *w* in 'were'. In pronouncing it, the lips need not necessarily be rounded.
       wakil, representative; **kawat,** wire; **kawin,** marry

y   is pronounced exactly like English *y* in 'year'.
       ya, yes; **kaya,** rich; **kayu,** wood

z   represents the same sound as the English *z* in 'zoo'.
       zat, substance; **ziarah,** pilgrimage; **izin,** permission
    Very often **z** is replaced by **j**, e.g. **izin →ijin; zaman →jaman.**

III Accent

The Indonesian language is weakly stressed. The stress accent in Indonesian is much weaker than in English. It is usually put on the last syllable.

gampáng	easy	**buku**	book
kepalá	head	**panglimá**	commander
laksamaná	admiral	**masyarakát**	society

Exercise 1

Read the following short sentences to practise your pronunciation. Mind the weak stress on the last syllable.

Saya sakit. Ini kuda. Apa itu? Hari dingin. Meréka tiba. Itu salah. Kapal itu berangkat. Siapa kamu? Ia guru. Jono belajar. Rumah ini kosong. Itu pertanyaan baik. Teman saya gembira.

Sekarang hari Sabtu. Ia mencari pekerjaan. Kami tinggal di sini. Kamu suka pisang? Kasim memukul anjing itu. Siapakah orang itu? Tuan Smith baru pulang.

ENGLISH VERSION

I am ill. This is a horse. What is that? It is cold (*lit.* The day is cold). They arrived. That is wrong. The boat is leaving. Who are you? He is a teacher. Jono is studying. This house is empty. That was a good question. My friend is happy. Today is Saturday. He is looking for a job. We live here. Do you like bananas? Kasim is beating the dog. Who is that man? Mr. Smith has just gone home.

CHAPTER 2

THE SIMPLE SENTENCE

The English verb has various forms. The verb 'to dance', for example, has the forms 'dance', 'dances', 'danced' and 'dancing'. We say 'I dance', 'Mary dances', 'They danced last night', 'The man is dancing'. We have conjugated the verb 'to dance' according to number, person and tense.

The Indonesian verb is not conjugated according to number, person and tense. Thus:

I laugh.	**Saya tertawa.**
Ali laughs.	**Ali tertawa.**
We laughed.	**Kami tertawa.**
The man is laughing.	**Orang itu tertawa.**
They were laughing.	**Meréka tertawa.**

The verb 'to be' in short sentences like 'I am ill', 'John was here', 'She is a nurse' can be left out in Indonesian.[1] We simply say 'I ill', 'John here', 'She nurse'. Thus:

I am tired.	**Saya lelah.**
John was in London.	**John di London.**
He is Mr. Allan.	**Ia Tuan Allan.**
That was wrong.	**Itu salah.**
Is this gold?	**Ini emas?**
You are first.	**Kamu pertama.**
What is this?	**Ini apa?**

In Indonesian there is no article corresponding exactly to the English article 'a'.[2]

---

[1] See also Chapter 31 on **ada** and **adalah.**
[2] See also Chapter 22, No. 2 on Numeral Coefficients.

A dog barks.	**Anjing menggonggong.**
A child cried.	**Anak menangis.**
A bird is singing.	**Burung menyanyi.**
I bought a pencil.	**Saya membeli pénsil.**
This is a hat.	**Ini topi.**
He is a teacher.	**Ia guru.**

The nearest equivalents to the English article 'the' are **ini** (this) and **itu** (that). They are put after the noun. Thus:

The (*or* this) trunk is heavy.	**Koper ini berat.**
The (*or* that) fire is burning.	**Api itu menyala.**
The (*or* this) pupil works hard.	**Murid ini bekerja keras.**
The (*or* that) cat ate the fish.	**Kucing itu makan ikan itu.**
He gave the (*or* this) picture to me.	**Ia memberi gambar ini pada saya.**

Exercise 2a

Combine words from column I with those from column II to make simple sentences.

(I)	(II)
mesin ini	**Rabu**
machine	Wednesday
pemburu itu	**mendapat coklat**
hunter	get chocolate
ini	**menggoréng ikan**
	fry fish
siapa	**datang dari London**
who	come from
Nyonya Jones	**Jalan Mawar**
Mrs.	Street Mawar
keréta-api itu	**menémbak harimau**
train	shoot tiger
tak seorang	**rusak**
nobody	out of order
ibu	**bénsin bukan minyak-tanah**
mother	benzine, not kerosene

itu   **kamu?**
                            you
serdadu   **kotor**
soldier   dirty
emas   **berangkat jam empat**
gold   start   o'clock four
hari ini   **menjawab**
today   answer
tiap anak   **bersaudara**
every child   brothers
air ini   **menangkap pencuri itu**
water   catch   thief
Ali dan Akhmad   **logam**
        and   metal

Vocabulary

pisau knife   **tua** old
mencuri to steal   **ular** snake
di sungai in the river **makan** to eat
pohon tree   **kambing** goat
tajam sharp   **ringan** light (not heavy)
loncéng clock   **babu** maid-servant
membuat to make   **sangat** very
dengan with   **berbisa** poisonous
rumput grass   **menjual** to sell
méja table   **terlalu** too
mandi to bathe   **cepat** fast
tidak not   **membunuh** to kill
bagus fine   **pisang** banana
kebun garden   **pagar** hedge

Exercise 2b

Translate the following sentences into English.

[1] Ia mencuri loncéng. [2] Kambing itu makan rumput. [3]
Méja ini ringan. [4] Pisau ini tidak tajam. [5] Akhmad membunuh

ular. [6] Pemburu itu mandi di sungai. [7] Loncéng ini terlalu cepat. [8] Babu itu memotong rumput dengan pisau. [9] Kebun ini sangat bagus. [10] Ali makan pisang. [11] Siapa membuat méja ini? [12] Itu pagar. [13] Pagar itu tidak bagus. [14] Ular ini berbisa. [15] Ia menjual kambing. [16] Babu itu sangat tua.

CHAPTER 3

ORDER OF WORDS

The order of words in an Indonesian sentence is like that of the English sentence.

Let us take a complete English sentence, e.g. 'The teacher reads a book'. When we compare this sentence with the Indonesian sentence, we shall see that the word order is alike, except for the place of **itu**.

The teacher/reads/a book.
Guru itu/membaca/buku.

When we insert adjectives or possessives in the English sentence we put them *before* the nouns. In the Indonesian sentence, however, we put the adjectives or possessives *after* the nouns.

The *young* TEACHER reads *my* BOOK.
GURU *muda* **itu membaca** BUKU *saya*.

Likewise:

This is a *difficult* PROBLEM.
Ini SOAL *sukar*.

That is *my* JACKET.
Itu JAKET *saya*.

A *mad* DOG bit the *blind* MAN.
ANJING *gila* **menggigit** ORANG *buta* **itu**.

Their HOUSE is near *our* SCHOOL.
RUMAH *mereka* **dekat** SEKOLAH *kami*.

In some cases English uses the word 'of' to show possession;
Indonesian does not have its equivalent.
Thus:

The leg of the table is broken.	**Kaki méja itu patah.**
He is pulling the tail of the dog.	**Ia menarik ékor anjing itu.**
The end of the story is sad.	**Akhir cerita itu sedih.**
Mr. Harold is the owner of this hotel.	**Tuan Harold pemilik hotél ini.**

The words **yang** (who, which) and **dan** (and) are used when
two adjectives qualify a noun.

a lovely, red flower	**bunga** *yang* **mérah** *dan* **indah** (*lit.* a flower which is red and lovely)
the strong, healthy man	**orang** *yang* **kuat** *dan* **séhat itu** (*lit.* the man who is strong and healthy)
the slender, strong branch of the tree	**dahan pohon** *yang* **ramping** *dan* **kuat itu** (*lit.* the branch of the tree which is slender and strong)

but:

the slender branch of the strong tree	**dahan ramping pohon kuat itu**

yang is also used when an adjective and a possessive qualify a
noun. The word order is always: noun-possessive–**yang**-adjective

rumah kami *yang* **baru**	our new house
arloji Anton *yang* **hilang**	Anton's lost watch
pintu rumah *yang* **kecil itu**	the small door of the house
but: **pintu rumah kecil itu**	the door of the small house

yang may be placed before any adjective to emphasize it.

anak *yang* **sakit**	a sick child
murid *yang* **malas itu**	the lazy pupil

Vocabulary

kursi chair	**pesawat-terbang** aeroplane
adik younger brother or sister	**meréka** they, their, them
kakak elder brother or sister	**sopir** chauffeur
nakal naughty	**pelaut** sailor
saya I, my, me	**kacamata** spectacles
dokter doctor	**terlambat** late
bambu bamboo	**memeriksa** to examine
bodoh stupid	**menangkap** to catch
pandai clever	**sangat** very
unta camel	**dinding** wall
listrik electricity	**mendarat** to land
mati off, out of action, dead	**polisi** police (man)
jurutik typist	**pencuri** thief
isteri wife	**hidung** nose
rajin diligent	**berdarah** to bleed
naik kelas to be promoted (at school)	**paman** uncle
	dokter-gigi dentist
negara country	**menarik** interesting
kaya rich	**gembira** happy

Exercise 3a

Translate the following into Indonesian

[1] This chair. [2] The clever doctor. [3] Our small house. [4] That is a camel. [5] My little (younger) brother is naughty. [6] This is a bamboo wall. [7] Our aeroplane is landing. [8] The electricity is off. [9] The doctor examined me. [10] That is interesting. [11] My spectacles are broken. [12] My elder sister was late. [13] This is the typist's chair. [14] Their chauffeur's wife was ill. [15] That man is a sailor. [16] The new typist is stupid.

Exercise 3b

Make sentences with the following words

[1] saya—ini—kakak
[2] murid—itu—rajin—naik kelas
[3] meréka—sangat—negara—kaya
[4] menangkap—polisi—itu—pencuri

[5] hidung—itu—berdarah—orang
[6] paman—dokter-gigi—Peter
[7] itu—menarik—film
[8] anak—sakit—Tuan Smith
[9] saya—ini—rumah
[10] dan—kuat—sehat—itu—orang—yang—gembira

CHAPTER 4

THE NEGATIVE SENTENCE

1   *The Negative Words* **tidak** *and* **bukan**
2   *The Negative Word* **belum**

The negative sentence is formed by putting **tidak** (not) before the
negated word, except when this word is a noun or pronoun in
which case **bukan** is used.

Tidak may also be replaced by **tiada** or **tak.**	
Ia *tidak* **datang.**	He did not come.
Meréka *tidak* **bahagia.**	They are not happy.
Suman di rumah? *Tidak.*	Is Suman in? No.
Ayah *tiada* **di sini.**	Father is not here.
Ini *tak* **gampang.**	This is not easy.

but: **Ia** *bukan* **tunangan saya**	He is not my fiancé.
Itu *bukan* **Salim.**	That was not Salim.
Bukan **kami yang** **menjerit.**	It was not us that shouted.
Ini pulpén Tuan? *Bukan*	Is this your fountain-pen? No.

'not yet' in Indonesian consists of only one word, **belum.** It is
used with any word and often forms a contrast with **sudah,** already.

Keréta-api *belum* **tiba.**	The train has not arrived yet.
Ibu Siti *belum* **sembuh.**	Siti's mother has not recovered yet.
Harimau itu *belum* **mati.**	The tiger is not yet dead.
Éddi sudah pulang? *Belum.*	Has Eddi come home yet? Not yet.
Oka *sudah* **membayar Tonitetapi** *belum* **membayar saya.**	Oka has already paid Toni, but has not paid me yet.

Exercise 4

Put the following in the negative by using tidak, tiada, tak, bukan *or* belum.

[1] Ibu menjemur pakaian. [2] Ali pergi ke sekolah. [3] Ayah membelikan saya sepasang sepatu. [4] Ini kemenakan saya. [5] Kamus ini mahal. [6] Orang itu Pak Hasan. [7] Kami sudah melihat film itu. [8] Saya suka tomat. [9] Nora yang merobék gambar itu. [10] Tetangga kami sudah kembali dari Éropa. [11] Suami saya di rumah. [12] Ini berlian. [13] Ia sudah menjual mesin-jahit itu. [14] Saya yang menyapa kamu di kantorpos.

ENGLISH VERSION OF THE NEGATIVE SENTENCES

[1] Mother did not hang the clothes to dry. [2] Ali did not go to school. [3] Father did not buy me a pair of shoes. [4] This is not my niece (nephew). [5] This dictionary is not expensive. [6] That man is not Pak Hasan. [7] We have not seen the film yet. [8] I do not like tomatoes. [9] It was not Nora who tore the picture. [10] Our neighbours have not returned from Europe yet. [11] My husband is not at home. [12] This is not diamond. [13] She has not sold the sewing-machine yet. [14] It was not I who spoke to you at the post-office.

CHAPTER 5

ASKING QUESTIONS

1 *The Suffix* **kah**
2 *The Question-tag* **bukan**

The interrogative form is quite simple. The English 'do' or 'does' in such forms as 'Do you swim?' 'Does Ali smoke?' 'Do they live here?' do not occur in Indonesian. There are three forms of asking questions in Indonesian.

1 The form: 'You swim?' 'Ali smoke?' 'They live here?' etc. Thus:

Do you swim?	**Kamu berenang?**
Does Ali smoke?	**Ali merokok?**
Do they live here?	**Meréka tinggal di sini?**
Did you call me?	**Kamu memanggil saya?**
Likewise:	
Is he ill?	**Ia sakit?**
Are you angry?	**Kamu marah?**
Is he a doctor?	**Ia dokter?**
Was everyone present?	**Semua hadir?**
Do not you dance?	**Kamu tidak berdansa?**
Did not he help them?	**Ia tidak menolong meréka?**
Were not they at home?	**Meréka tidak di rumah?**

2 By putting the question-word *apa* (what) or *apakah* (what) at the beginning of the question.

Apa(kah) ia tahu?	Does he know?
Apa(kah) ini cuka?	Is this vinegar?
Apa(kah) kamu gila?	Are you crazy?
Apa(kah) itu rumah meréka?	Is that their house?

3 The form with the suffix **-kah,** which is attached to the word that demands an answer. The suffixed word usually opens the sentence.

Bukankah ia ahli-hukum?	Is not he a solicitor?
Sudahkah anak itu mandi?	Has the child already taken a bath?
Maukah kamu datang?	Will you come?
Betulkah meréka sudah berangkat?	Is it true that they have (already) left?

Note: Form 1 and form 2 are used in spoken Indonesian. Form 3 is formal.

To turn statements into questions that need not be answered English uses the question-tag 'aren't you?', 'don't you?', 'hasn't he?', 'did she?', etc. There is only one question-tag in Indonesian, **bukan?**

Kamu kenal pada Sumi, bukan?	You know Sumi, don't you?
Jono tidak terlambat, bukan?	Jono wasn't late, was he?
Ia orang Inggeris, bukan?	He is an Englishman, isn't he?
Ibu akan membuat kué, bukan?	Mother will make a cake, won't she?

Exercise 5

Make up questions to which the following are the answers. Use all three forms.

1 .... **Ya, saya kenal padanya**   Yes, I know him.
2 .... **Tidak, saya tidak haus**   No, I am not thirsty.
3 .... **Ya, meréka gembira**   Yes, they are happy.
4 .... **Bukan, ini bukan tas ayah saya**   No, this is not my father's bag.
5 .... **Ya, anak ini pandai**   Yes, this child is clever.
6 .... **Belum, ibunya belum sembuh**   No, her mother has not recovered yet.
7 .... **Tidak, kami tidak mau pergi dengan kamu**   No, we will not go with you.
8 .... **Betul, saya dokter**   That is right, I am a doctor.
9 .... **Bukan, Pak Amat bukan tukang-kebun**   No, Pak Amat is not a gardener.
10 .... **Sudah, saya sudah makan**   Yes, I have already eaten.

CHAPTER 6

PRONOUNS

The Personal Pronouns are:

SAYA or **aku**	I
kamu or **engkau**	you
IA or **DIA** or **BELIAU**	he, she
KAMI or **KITA**	we
MEREKA	they

Note: Acceptable forms are shown in CAPITALS.

SAYA is used when we speak to our superiors, to our equals and to our subordinates. It is also used by teachers when they speak to their pupils.

aku is familiar, and it is used in stories (colloquially and in first person narrative) and used among boys and by parents when they speak to their children; it is generally used in speaking to servants.

kamu (singular and plural) is used by teachers to address their pupils, it is a form used among schoolboys, and may be used as a form of address to servants.

engkau has become obsolete (cf. English 'thee').

IA (he, she) when stressed becomes **DIA**.

BELIAU is used for persons of high rank, persons we pay respect to.

KAMI is 'we' excluding the person spoken to.

KITA is 'we' including the person spoken to.

Thus, an Indonesian might say to an Englishman: '**Kami** memproklamirkan kemerdékaan kami dalam tahun 1945'. (We proclaimed our independence in 1945.)

But he must say: '**Kita** hidup dalam abad keduapuluh'. (We live in the twentieth century.)

A married woman is addressed as **Nyonya** (plural **Nyonya-Nyonya**), an unmarried woman as **Nona** (plural **Nona-Nona**). A man is addressed aş **Tuan** or **Saudara** (plural **Tuan-Tuan** or **Saudara-Saudara**). An elderly woman is addressed as **Ibu** (plural **Ibu-Ibu**) and an elderly man as **Pak** or **Bapak** (plural **Bapak-Bapak**).

It is customary to address a person with his name as well and use it during the course of the conversation as substitute for 'you'. So, when one knows an elderly man by the name of Pangkat, one should address him with '**Pak** Pangkat'.

Pak Pangkat akan ke mana?	Where are you going?
Ini cucu Pak Pangkat?	Is this your grandchild?
Oh, ia belum membayar Pak Pangkat?	Oh, has not he paid you yet?

Speaking to one's equals, friends, relatives and children one usually makes use of the name, title or the occupation of the person addressed.

to Létta:	**Létta sudah melihat film Ben Hur?**	Have you already seen Ben Hur?
to a priest:	**Pastor suka téh atau kopi?**	Do you like tea or coffee?
to a doctor:	**Boléhkah saya menilpon dokter?**	Can I give you a ring?

The English 'it' for animals and things does not exist in Indonesian. The animal or thing is mentioned throughout. See also note on **nya** below.

Sri has a monkey; it is a funny animal	**Sri mempunyai kera; kera itu binatang lucu.**
The bus plunged into a ravine; it carried forty passengers.	**Bis itu terjun ke jurang; bis itu mengangkut empatpuluh penumpang.**

We saw that the possessive is put after the noun. Notice that the possessives **ku** (my), **mu** (your) and **nya** (his, her) are attached to the noun. Thus:

topi saya, topiku	my hat	**rumah kami**	our house
rapormu	your report	**dunia kita**	our world
rambutnya	her hair, his hair	**makanan meréka**	their food

ku, mu, nya are also attached to prepositions, e.g.

kepadaku	to me
di mukamu	before you
oléhnya	by him, by her

nya may be used as object for persons or things. Thus:

Ia memukul saya (aku)	He hit me
Saya melihat kamu	I saw you
Kamu mencintai dia? or **mencintainya?**	Do you love him, her?
Ia mengetahuinya	He knew it
Meréka telah mengundang kami	They have invited us (excluding the person spoken to!)
Siapa memanggil kita?	Who is calling us? (including the person spoken to!)
Jangan bergaul dengan meréka	Don't associate with them

The English *possessives* 'mine', 'yours', 'hers', 'John's', etc. are rendered by the word **punya**. It is always placed before the possessive.

Mantel ini punya saya (punyaku)	This coat is mine
Ini punyamu?	Is this yours?
Sepéda itu bukan punyanya	That bicycle is not his, hers
Ya, itu punya kami	Yes, that is ours
Bukan, tanah ini bukan punya meréka	No, this land is not theirs
Jas-hujan ini punya Ari	This mackintosh is Ari's (In English we prefer to say: This is Ari's mackintosh)

The *emphatic pronouns* 'myself', 'yourself', 'ourselves', etc. are represented by **sendiri.**[1]

Saya sendiri melihatnya	I saw him (her, it) myself
Ia sendiri mengatakan begitu	He himself (she herself) said so
Kami dapat mengerjakannya sendiri	We can do it ourselves
Meréka sendiri berbuat demikian	They themselves did so

Note: Although the forms **kamu** and **mu** will be found in this book, it should be remembered that these forms are supplied for the sake of brevity and that the learner is recommended to use the other second personal pronouns: **Tuan, Saudara, Nyonya, Pak,** etc.

The use of **aku** and **ku** is strongly discouraged.

The *indefinite pronouns* are:

orang, one, man, people; **seseorang,** somebody; **salah seorang,** (some)one; **barangsiapa,** who; **siapa-siapa,** whoever; **masing-masing,** each; **sesuatu, apa-apa,** something; **tak suatupun,** nothing; **segala sesuatu,** everything.

Orang harus mati	Man must die
Seseorang telah memetik bunga mawar kita	Somebody has picked our roses
Salah seorang dari kita harus minta pertolongan	One of us has to ask for help
Masing-masing mendapat hadiah	Each got a present
Ada sesuatuyang akan saya tanyakan kepadamu	There is something I want to ask you about
Rupanya ada apa-apa di situ	There seems to be something going on over there
Tak sesuatupun sempurna	Nothing is perfect

---

[1] **sendiri** also means 'own' and 'alone', e.g.

Itu mobilnya sendiri	That is his own car.
Itu salahmu sendiri	That is your own fault.
Ia pergi sendiri (or **sendirian**).	He went alone.
Orang itu berjalan sendiri (or **sendirian**).	That man walked alone

Conversational Expressions

Selamat pagi	Good morning
Selamat siang	Good afternoon
Selamat malam	Good evening, or good night
Apa kabar?	How are you? (*lit.* What news)
Baik or **Kabar baik**	Good (*lit.* Good news)
Terima kasih	Thank you
Terima kasih banyak	Thank you very much
Selamat makan	Good appetite
Selamat tidur	Sleep well
Selamat	Congratulations
Selamat jalan	Good-bye (Safe journey, said to persons who are leaving)
Selamat tinggal	Good-bye (said to persons one is taking leave of)
Sampai bertemu lagi	Au revoir, Auf Wiedersehen
Mari masuk	Come in
Silakan masuk	Come in, please
Selamat datang	Welcome
Maafkan	Excuse me
Permisi	Excuse me (said when one wants to enter or leave somebody else's house)
Mari kita pergi	Let us go

CHAPTER 7

QUESTION-WORDS

Question-words are put either at the beginning or at the end of the question. They are:

siapa	Who
apa	What
kapan or **bilamana**	When
mana or **di mana**	Where
ke mana	Where to
dari mana	Where from
mana	Which
bagaimana or **berapa**	How
mengapa or **apa sebabnya**	Why

To emphasize the question-word the suffix **-kah** is attached to it. When the question-word is put at the end of the sentence, **-kah** is usually left out.

Siapa kamu?
Siapakah kamu?
Kamu siapa? } Who are you?

Di mana kamu tinggal?
Di manakah kamu tinggal?
Kamu tinggal di mana? } Where do you live?

Bilamana ia tiba?
Kapankah ia tiba?
Ia tiba kapan? } When did he arrive?

where The difference between **mana** and **di mana.** When one is asked a question with **mana** one is expected to show or produce the object asked for.

A guard might ask a passenger **Mana karcis Tuan?** (Your ticket, please?) The passenger must, of course, produce his ticket out of his pocket and hand it to the guard. It would be silly for the passenger to say **Di saku saya** (It is in my pocket).

'**Mana bukumu?**' '**Oh, saya lupa membawanya.**'
'Where is your book?' 'Oh, I've forgotten to bring it.'

di mana asks after the place or the position of the object in question. The teacher asks: '**Di mana bulan?**' (Where is the moon?) and the pupils answer: '**Di langit.**' (In the sky).

'**Di mana ia sekarang?**' '**Ia di kamarnya.**' 'Where is he now?' 'He is in his room.'

ke mana, to what place, to which place:

Ke mana ia pergi?	Where did he go to?
Bis ini menuju ke mana?	Where is this bus heading for?

Often the verb is left out: **Meréka ke mana?** Where are they going to?

dari mana, from what place, from which place
Dari mana kamu datang?	Where do you come from?
Badut itu muncul dari mana?	Where did the clown appear from?

The verb is often left out: **Ia dari mana?** Where is she from?

how   There are two Indonesian 'hows' viz. **bagaimana,** in what manner, by what means; and **berapa,** to what extent or degree.

Bagaimana kita dapat menjadi kaya?	How can we get rich?
Berapa panjang tampar ini?	How long is this rope?

who   is **siapa;** before a verb it is **siapa yang.** The elements of **siapa yang** may be separated from each other and **siapa** put at the end of the question.

Who was that?	**Siapa itu?** or **Itu siapa?**
Who pays?	**Siapa yang membayar?** or **Yang membayar siapa?**

whose *followed* by a noun is **siapa** *preceded* by the noun

Whose book is this?	**Buku siapa ini?** or **Ini buku siapa?**
Whose house is that?	**Rumah siapa itu?** or **Itu rumah siapa?**
but: Whose is it?	**Punya siapa ini?** or **Ini punya siapa?**

which is **mana yang** or **yang mana**. When put at the end of the question it is always **yang mana**

Which does he choose?	**Mana yang ia pilih?** or **Ia pilih yang mana?**
Which is better?	**Mana yang lebih baik?** or **Lebih baik yang mana?**

which *followed* by a noun is **mana** or **yang mana** preceded by the noun

Which house?	**Rumah mana?**
Which man?	**Orang yang mana?**
but: Which one?	**Yang mana?**

what is **apa yang**. **apa** may be separated from **yang** and put at the end of the question.

What did you hear?	**Apa yang kamu dengar?** or **Yang kamu dengar apa?**
What is he doing?	**Apa yang ia kerjakan?** or **Yang ia kerjakan apa?**
but:	
What is it (this)?	**Apa ini?** or **Ini apa?**
What is that?	**Apa itu?** or **Itu apa?**

what *followed* by a noun is **apa** *preceded* by the noun

What man is he?	**Orang apa ia?** or **Ia orang apa?**
What book is this?	**Buku apa ini?** or **Ini buku apa?**

Note:

What is your name?	**Siapa** (not **apa**) **namamu?**
What time?	**Jam berapa?** (not **apa**)
Where do you live?	**Kamu tinggal di mana?** or
	Rumahmu di mana?
	(*lit.* Where is your house?)

Exercise 7a

Make up two forms of questions to which the following are the answers:

1 .... **Itu jakét saya**   That is my jacket.
2 .... **Ia tinggal dekat geréja**   He lives near the church.
3 .... **Karena perempuan itu sedih**   Because the woman is sad.
4 .... **Tinggi menara itu seratus méter**   The tower is a hundred metres high.
5 .... **Saya makan kacang**   I am eating peanuts.
6 .... **Namanya Mirna**   Her name is Mirna.
7 .... **Mantel ini punya ibu Dora**   It is the coat of Dora's mother.
8 .... **Minggu depan meréka pindah**   They move next week.
9 .... **Bukan, lusa bukan hari-libur**   No, the day after to-morrow is not a holiday.
10 .... **Ini buku sejarah**   This is a history book.
11 .... **Ya, itu punya saya**   Yes, that is mine.
12 .... **Orang itu paman Badri**   That man is Badri's uncle.
13 .... **Harga lampu ini limapuluh rupiah**   The price of this lamp is fifty rupiahs.
14 .... **Ini!**   Here it is!
15 .... **Ayah saya pergi ke Tokyo bulan yang lalu**   My father went to Tokyo last month.
16 .... **Kami tiba jam tujuh**   We arrived at seven o'clock.

Exercise 7b

Answer the following questions in Indonesian:

1 **Dapatkah kamu menyanyi?**   Can you sing?
2 **Apakah ibukota Perancis?**   What is the capital of France?

3 **Kamu dapat berbahasa Indonésia?** Do (can) you speak Indonesian?

4 **Mengapa kamu tidak masuk kerja?** Why did not you come to work?

5 **Berapa umurmu?** How old are you?

6 **Mengapa kamu tidak merokok?** Why do not you smoke?

7 **Di mana saya dapat membeli perangko?** Where can I buy stamps?

8 **Siapa memotong rambutmu?** Who cuts your hair?

9 **Kamu menulis dengan apa?** What do you write with?

10 **Jam berapa pertunjukan mulai?** What time does the performance start?

11 **Pencopét itu lari ke mana?** Where did the pickpocket run to?

12 **Apa yang kamu baca di suratkabar?** What did you read in the newspaper?

13 **Lasmi mau minta apa?** What does Lasmi want?

14 **Payung siapa ini?** Whose umbrella is this?

15 **Kamu membeli cincin yang mana?** Which ring did you buy?

16 **Berapa kali ia memukul kamu?** How many times did he beat you?

Vocabulary

Paris Paris
karena because (of)
duapuluh lima twenty-five
tahun year
dapat can
menyebabkan to cause
kangker cancer
di at, in
kantorpos post-office
di kantorpos at the post-office
**tukang-potong-rambut,
  tukang-pangkas** barber

pulpén fountain-pen
jam delapan (at) eight o'clock
ke to
gang alley
berita news
tentang about
pembunuhan murder
és ice
berlian diamond
tiga kali three times

CHAPTER 8

TENSES

As you have already seen, the Indonesian verb is not conjugated according to number, person or tense. However, there are means to express the tenses.

The **future** is indicated by **mau** (want, will, shall), **akan** (will, shall) or **hendak** (wish, will, shall)

Tuan Hadi akan pulang jam lima.	Mr. Hadi will come home at five o'clock.
Keluarga itu akan pergi ke Hongkong	That family will go to Hongkong.
Saya hendak tidur.	I will go to sleep.
Ia mau datang.	He will come.

The **continuous tense** may be indicated by **sedang, masih** or **lagi**

Ayah masih mandi.	Father is having a bath.
Darmo sedang makan.	Darmo is eating.
Ia lagi menyeberang jalan ketika ia melihat temannya.	He was crossing the street when he saw his friend.

The **past** may be indicated by a specific adverb or adverbial phrase of time e.g. **kemarin** (yesterday), **minggu yang lalu** (last week). The adverb of time can be put at the beginning or at the end of the sentence or after the subject.

Kemarin saya jatuh dari tangga	⎫
Saya jatuh dari tangga kemarin	⎬ I fell from the ladder yesterday.
Saya kemarin jatuh dari tangga	⎭
Minggu yang lalu meréka kawin.	⎫
Meréka kawin minggu yang lalu.	⎬ They married last week.
Meréka minggu yang lalu kawin.	⎭

Dahulu kami tinggal di Manila. **Kami tinggal di Manila dahulu.** **Kami dahulu tinggal di Manila.**	We used to live in Manilla (*lit.* Formerly we lived in Manilla).

The **perfect tense** may be indicated by **telah** (already), **sudah** (already) or **baru** (just).

Orang sakit itu telah sembuh.		The sick man has recovered.
Tuan Fry sudah kembali ke Inggeris.	Completed actions	Mr. Fry has returned to England.
Adik saya baru bangun.		My little brother has just woken up.

Vocabulary

memikirkan to think of
soal problem
terbang to fly
tamu guest
mengendarakan to drive
menggigit to bite
tiga bulan lagi in three months
dua minggu yang lalu a fortnight ago
(di) dalam in (side)
kemarin malam last night
bulan depan next month
bésok soré tomorrow afternoon
nanti malam tonight
kemarin dahulu the day before yesterday
meninggal (dunia) to die
dua tahun yang lalu two years ago

pada suatu hari one day
pada suatu waktu once
berbaring to lie, to recline
di bawah under
berdoa to pray
tangga steps
menyelesaikan to finish
pekerjaan work
penulis, sékretaris secretary
sekarang now
mengerti to understand
baru-baru ini recently
gigi tooth, teeth
bercakap to talk
dari from
berjalan to walk
duduk to sit
pintu door
menutup to close
mobil motor-car

Exercise 8

Translate the following into Indonesian:

[1] She is thinking of the problem. [2] Mr. Lim will fly to Bangkok next month. [3] Our guest is talking with my father. [4] He has said his prayers. [5] You did not close the door last night. [6] The cat is lying under the table. [7] He died a fortnight ago. [8] Who drove the motor-car? [9] I shall think of it. [10] She saw her friend the day before yesterday. [11] He did not understand it. [12] We bite with our teeth. [13] They are walking under the tree now. [14] We married two years ago. [15] I sat in the car this morning. [16] My secretary will go home in three months. [17] One day our driver fell from the steps. [18] I shall finish the work next month.

CHAPTER 9

VERBS

Introductory

An Indonesian verb normally has the following forms:

1 The root word: **lalu** (go through), **gambar** (picture), **tinggi** (high).
2 Prefix + the root: **berlalu** (go through), **menggambar** (draw), **mempertinggi** (heighten).
3 Prefix + the root + suffix: **melalui** (go through something), **menggambarkan** (illustrate), **mempertinggikan** (heighten).

The root of the verb may be a verb, a noun, an adjective, etc. The functions of the prefixes **ber-, me-, memper-** and the suffixes **-kan, -i** will be discussed in the next chapters.

CHAPTER 10

VERBS (Continued)

The Prefix ber-

When the root word begins with **r** the prefix **ber** drops its **r**

rumah	(house)	**berumah**	to reside
rasa	(feeling)	**berasa**	to feel
rotan	(cane)	**berotan**	to look for cane

ber also drops its **r** in **bekerja**, to work; from **kerja**, work.

ber becomes **bel** in **belajar**, to learn; from **ajar**, teaching.

The meaning of verbs with ber-

1 *To denote a possession*[1]

rambut hair **Ia berambut pirang.** She has blonde hair.

anak child **Meréka beranak banyak.** They have many children.

2 *to wear*

baju blouse **Gadis itu berbaju mérah.** That girl wears a red blouse.

kacamata spectacles **Umar berkacamata.** Umar wears spectacles.

3 *to go by any vehicle*[2]

sépeda bicycle **Saya bersepéda ke sekolah.** I cycle to school.

keréta-api train **Kami berkeréta-api ke Malang.** We went by train to Malang.

---

[1] 'to have, to own, to possess' is **mempunyai**. Thus:
Ia berambut pirang = Ia mempunyai rambut pirang.
Meréka beranak banyak = Meréka mempunyai banyak anak.

[2] Colloquially, **naik** is used, e.g.
Saya naik bis. I went by bus.
Ia naik keréta-api. He went by train.

4 *to act the part of*

guru teacher   **Ia bukan guru, tetapi sering berguru.**
He is not a teacher, but he often acts as a teacher.

tukang workman   **Pamannya bertukang.** Her uncle
is a workman (*lit.* Her uncle works as a workman).

5 *What one does for one's living, occupation:*

kebun kelapa coconut plantation   **Ia berkebun kelapa.**
He owns a coconut-plantation.

jual sell;   **buah-buahan** fruit   **Orang ini berjual**
buah-buahan. This man sells fruit.

6 *to involve oneself with others, reciprocal action:*

(often the suffix **-an** is added, sometimes the root word is
duplicated)

salam greeting, handshake   **Kami bersalaman.** We
shook hands.

pukul hit   **Kedua anak laki-laki itu berpukul-puku-**
lan. The two boys hit each other.

7 *to do something for oneself*

cukur shave   **Pak Hassan sedang bercukur.** Pak
Hassan is shaving himself.

hias apply make-up   **Ia berhias di muka cermin.**
She made up before the mirror.

8 *to hold, to celebrate an event*

puasa fast   **Siapa berpuasa?** Who is fasting?

ulang-tahun birthday   **Nora berulang-tahun hari ini.**
It is Nora's birthday today.

9 *to obtain, to achieve*

hasil success, gain   **Ia berhasil mencari ramuan itu.**
He succeeded in finding the herb.

hadiah prize   **Siapa berhadiah pertama?** Who got
the first prize?

10 *to utter*

kata word **Saya berkata, 'Tidak'.** I said, 'No'.
sorak shout **Meréka bersorak, 'Hidup'.** They shouted, 'Hurray'.

11 *to perform the action implicit in the root word* (cf. English: gamble →
to gamble; dance →to dance).

judi gamble **Meréka berjudi sehari semalam.**
They gambled night and day.
sandiwara play **Katrin pandai bersandiwara.**
Katrin is good at acting.

12 *to denote the indefiniteness of a multitude* (usually the suffix **-an is**
attached to emphasize it)

gemerlap twinkle **Ribuan bintang bergemerlapan
di langit.** Thousands of stars twinkle in the sky.
hambur scatter **Kertas-kertas berhamburan di
lantai.** Paper of all sorts lay scattered on the floor.

13 *to make use of*

layar sail **Kita berlayar ke pulau Madura.** We
sailed to the island of Madura (*lit.* We used a sail).
bahasa language **Kamu berbahasa Inggeris?** Do
you speak English? (*lit.* Can you use the English language as
a means of communication?)

When the root word is a numeral, **ber-** *denotes a 'oneness'*

satu one **Marilah kita bersatu.** Let us unite.
tiga three **Perampok itu bertiga.** There were three
robbers.

When the root word is a verb, **ber-** *has no function at all*

lalu or **berlalu** to go through, to pass **Ia (ber)-lalu di
muka rumah saya.** He went past my house.
baring or **berbaring** to lie, to recline **Pemalas itu
sedang (ber)-baring di ranjangnya.** That lazy fellow is
lying in his bed.

belanja or **berbelanja** to go shopping   **Ibu (ber)-belanja sepanjang pagi.** Mother has been shopping all morning.

pindah or **berpindah** to move   **Meréka telah (ber)-pindah ke kota.** They have moved to the city.

Vocabulary

nénék	grandmother	**tukar**	change
kakék	grandfather	**tempat-duduk**	seat
gigi	tooth, teeth	**orang-désa**	villager
tepuktangan	clap	**jagung**	corn
janji	promise	**tanam**	plant
mengulangi	to repeat	**luka**	wound
pakaian	clothes	**perampok**	robber
darah	blood	**hadirin**	audience
empat	four	**biru**	blue
telur	egg	**cium**	kiss
selisih	quarrel	**sering**	often
riuh-rendah	boisterously	**hadirin**	audience
kekejaman	cruelty		

Exercise 10

*Add the prefix **ber-** to the words in parentheses and translate the sentences:*

- [1] *Nenek tiada (gigi).*
- [2] *Kami (mobil) ke Padang.*
- [3] *Hadirin (tepuktangan) riuh-rendah.*
- [4] *Ia (janji) tidak akan mengulangi kekejaman itu.*
- [5] *Gadis itu suka (pakaian) biru.*
- [6] *Didi dan saya telah (tukar) tempat-duduk.*
- [7] *Ayam ini tidak (telur) hari ini.*
- [8] *Kedua perempuan itu (cium).*
- [9] *Orang-desa itu (tanam) jagung.*
- [10] *Lukanya (darah).*
- [11] *Perampok itu (empat).*
- [12] *Mengapa kamu sering (selisih)?*

CHAPTER 11

VERBS (Continued)

The Prefix me-

Verbs with the prefix **me-** are either transitive, i.e. they take objects, or intransitive, i.e. they do not take objects. Unlike **ber-** the prefix **me-** can become **men, meng, mem, meny.**

It becomes **men** when the root word starts with **d, j, c** or **t.**

duga	menduga	to suspect
jadi	menjadi	to become
cari	mencari	to look for
tarik	menarik	to pull
	(**t** drops)	

Exception: **terjemah** **menterjemahkan** to translate

It becomes **meng** when the root word starts with a vowel or with **h, g** or **k.**

ambil	mengambil	to take
harap	mengharap	to hope
gunting	menggunting	to cut (with scissors)
kirim	mengirim	to send
	(**k** drops)	

It becomes **mem** when the root word starts with **b** or **p.**

buru	memburu	to hunt, to pursue
pukul	memukul	to hit
	(**p** drops)	
Exceptions: punya	mempunyai	to have, to own, to possess
peduli	mempedulikan	to care[1]

[1] **Saya tidak peduli** I am indifferent.

It becomes **meny** when the root word starts with **s.**

siksa	**menyiksa** (s drops)	to torture
sapu	**menyapu** (s drops)	to sweep

The meaning of verbs with *me* —

1 *When the root word is a noun* **me-** *denotes:*

(*a*) that the act is done by means of the tools, implements, instruments, etc. indicated in the root word

gunting scissors **Gadis itu menggunting kain itu.** The girl cut the cloth.

sapu broom **Kamu sudah menyapu kamarmu?** Have you swept your room?

(*b*) that the act is done with the material, substance, etc. indicated in the root word

kapur lime **Tukang-kapur itu sedang mengapur dinding itu.** The white-washer is whitewashing the wall.

cat (cét) paint **Saya menyuruh dia mencat garasi** I let him paint the garage.

(*c*) the making of the comestible indicated in the root word

roti bread **Ibu sedang meroti.** Mother is making bread.

gulai soup **Koki kemarin menggulai ayam.** The cook was making chicken soup yesterday.

(*d*) going to the place indicated in the root word

darat land **Kami mendarat di pulau yang tak berpenduduk.** We landed in an uninhabited island.

tepi side **Mobil kecil itu menepi ketika ada sebuah truk besar mendatang.** The small car moved aside when a large truck approached.

(e) the characteristic action of the thing indicated in the root word

babi buta blind pig **Janganlah membabi-buta!** Don't act blindly!

semut ant **Orang-orang menyemut ketika ada kecelakaan di muka rumah saya.** People crowded round when there was an accident in front of my house.

(f) the production of the sound indicated in the root word

aum roar **Harimau mengaum.** Tigers roar.

cicit squeak **Tikus mencicit.** Mice squeak.

2 *When the root word is an adjective* **me-** *denotes that the subject taking on the quality of the root word*

mérah red **Opsir itu marah; mukanya memérah.** The officer was angry; his face turned red (reddened).

hébat violent **Badai menghébat.** The storm became violent.

3 *When the root word is a verb, it is the form with* **me-** *which is normally used*

goréng fry **Ia menggoréng telur.** She fried an egg.

bawa bring, take **Saya lupa membawa payung.** I forgot to bring an umbrella.

The following verb-roots never take the prefix **ber-** *or* **me-**

akan	will, shall	**mati**	die
mau	want, will, shall	**menang**	win
hendak	wish, will, shall	**minta**	ask
ambruk	collapse	**minum**	drink
antri	queue	**mogok**	strike
apal or **hafal**	know by heart	**mohon**	beg
bangkit	rise	**mungkir**	deny
bangun	wake	**mundur**	retreat
bimbang	doubt	**mungkin**	might
bisa	can	**muncul**	appear
bubar	disperse	**naik**	ascend

dapat	can	**omong**	talk
datang	come	**pergi**	go
jatuh	fall	**perlu**	need
duduk	sit	**percaya**	believe
gagal	fail	**pulang**	go home
harus	must	**sampai**	arrive
hidup	live	**setuju**	agree
ikut	join	**suka**	like
ingat	remember	**tahu**	know
ingin	long	**tamat**	finish
insaf	realize	**tampil**	come forward
kalah	lose	**terbang**	fly
kawin	marry	**tertawa**	laugh
kemari	come here	**tetap**	remain
lenyap	disappear	**téwas**	perish
léwat	pass, go through	**tiba**	arrive
lolos	flee	**tidur**	sleep
lulus	pass (an exam.)	**tinggal**	stay
lupa	forget	**turun**	descend
maju	advance	**turut**	go with
makan	eat		(someone)
mandi	bath	**tak usah**	need not
mangkat	decease (of noblemen)	**wafat**	decease (of holy people)

Note: **bangun, dapat, datang, ikut, kalah, tetap, tinggal, turun, turut** may be prefixed **me-**. However, they then have a completely different meaning.

membangun	to build	**menetap**	to settle
mendapat	to get	**meninggal**	
mendatang	to approach	**(dunia)**	to die
mengikut	to follow	**menurun**	to copy, to decline
mengalah	to yield	**menurut**	to obey

Thus:

Saya bangun jam enam.   I get up at six o'clock.
Saya yang membangun sekolah itu.   It was I who built that school.

Kamu dapat menggambar gajah? Can you draw an
elephant?
Kamu mendapat tujuh untuk ulanganmu. You got seven
for your repetition.
Mardi tetap tenang. Mardi remained calm.
Keluarga itu telah menetap di Kanada. That family have
settled in Canada.
Ia tinggal di désa. He lived in a village.
Ia meninggal di désa. He died in a village.

Vocabulary

(di)dalam in	**surat** letter
baca to read	**bunuh** to kill
suratkabar newspaper	**anjing** dog
mudah easy	**gila** mad
gergaji saw	**seberang** opposite side
balok beam	**hujan** rain
besar big	**pada** at
dengar to hear	**tukang-kapur** whitewasher
deru howling	**seseorang** somebody
di hutan in the forest	**dinding** wall
tulis to write	**kotor** dirty
(ke) pada to	**pésta** feast, party
bibi aunt	**awan** cloud
dengan selamat safely	**uang** money
melalui through	**cuci** to wash
nyanyi to sing	**hitam** black
tari to dance	**rokok** cigarette
angin wind	**sebentar lagi** soon
simpan to keep	

Exercise 11

Add the prefix **me-** *(mind its changes) to the words in parentheses and translate the sentences:*

[1] Ayah sedang (baca) suratkabar.
[2] Tidak mudah (gergaji) balok besar ini.
[3] Kami (dengar) angin (deru) melalui pohon-pohon di hutan.
[4] Poppi (tulis) surat kepada bibinya.

[5] Seseorang telah (bunuh) anjing gila itu.
[6] Tukang-kapur sedang (kapur) dinding kotor itu.
[7] Kapal-terbang kami (darat) dengan selamat di Karaci.
[8] Kamu harus (simpan) uangmu dalam laci.
[9] Ia duduk (rokok) di bawah pohon.
[10] Meréka (nyanyi) dan (tari) pada pésta itu.
[11] Babu kemarin tidak (cuci) pakaian.
[12] Awan (hitam), sebentar lagi akan hujan.
[13] Mari kita (seberang).
[14] Ia tidak mau (jawab) pertanyaan itu.

CHAPTER 12

VERBS (Continued)

1   *The Combination of the Prefix* **me-** *and the Suffix* **-i**
2   *The Combination of the Prefix* **me-** *and the Suffix* **-kan**

1 Verbs with the Prefix me- and the Suffix -i are always transitive

1 *When the root word is a verb the combination* **me + i** *denotes:*

(*a*) the occupation of a seat, a place, a position

duduk sit   **Musuh telah menduduki kota.** The enemy has occupied the town.

diam stay   **Siapa mendiami rumah itu?** Who occupies that house?

(*b*) repetition of an action

tampar slap   **Ia menampari isterinya.** He slapped his wife (repeatedly).

tendang kick   **Ali menendangi anjing itu.** Ali kicked the dog (repeatedly).

(*c*) the elimination of the distance between the subject and the object, i.e. the action can be said to be spatially situated with the object

terbang fly   **Pesawat itu menerbangi desa kami.** The plane flew over our village.

lompat jump   **Mereka melompati selokan itu.** They jumped over the gutter.

2 *When the root word is a noun* **me + i** *denotes:*

(*a*) the disposal of the thing indicated in the root word

bulu feather   **Babu sedang membului ayam.** The servant is plucking a chicken.

sisik scale   **Ia menyisiki ikan dengan pisau besar.** She scaled a fish with a big knife.

(b) *the provision of the thing indicated in the root word*

genting tile   **Tukang itu menggentingi atap.** The workman is putting tiles on the roof.

kancing button   **Perempuan itu mengancingi keméja suaminya.** The woman sewed buttons on her husband's shirt.

(c) an often figurative extension of the idea indicated in the root word

teman friend   **Marilah kita menemani Olli ke setasiun.** Let us accompany Olli to the station.

jago champion   **Ia menjagoi lapangan.** He excels at the (sport) field.

2 The combination Prefix me- and Suffix -kan always makes transitive verbs

1 *When the root word is a verb* **me** + **kan** *denotes:*

(a) the causative form of the root word

kibar wave   **Kami mengibarkan bendéra.** We hoisted the flag (*lit.* We made the flag wave).

jatuh fall   **Pemain itu menjatuhkan bola.** The player dropped the ball.

(b) doing something for someone

beli buy   **Sari membelikan adiknya permén.** Sari bought candy for her little brother.

buka open   **Saya membukakan tamu pintu.** I opened the door for the guest.

(c) doing something with the object mentioned

tikam stab   **Ia menikamkan keris.** He stabbed with a keris.

témbak shoot   **Meréka menémbakkan meriam.** They fired the cannon.

(*d*) that the object mentioned is the cause of the action indicated in the root word

tertawa laugh **Murid-murid itu menertawakan lelucon itu.** The pupils laughed at the anecdote (*lit.* The anecdote caused them laugh).

tangis cry **Gadis kecil itu sedang menangiskan bonéka.** The little girl was crying for a doll.

(*e*) a corresponding action

séwa rent, let **Ia menyéwakan rumahnya untuk lima bulan.** He let his house for five months.

but: **Kami menyéwa banglo.** We rent a bungalow.

pinjam borrow, lend **Dapatkah kamu meminjamkan saya seratus rupiah?** Could you lend me hundred rupiahs?

but: **Boléhkah saya meminjam mesintikmu?** May I borrow your typewriter?

dengar hear, listen **Kami mendengarkan musik di radio.** We listened to the music on the radio.

but: **Saya tidak mendengar apa-apa.** I did not hear anything.

lihat see, watch **Guru melihatkan murid-murid bermain.** The teacher watched the pupils playing.

but: **Kita melihat dengan mata kita.** We see with our eyes.

2 *When the root word is an adjective,* **me+kan** *denotes that the object mentioned is taking in the state indicated in the root word*

gelap dark **Tuan Moran menggelapkan kamar karena ia akan mempertunjukkan film.** Mr. Moran darkened the room as he wanted to show a film.

hilang lost **Ia menghilangkan cincinnya.** She has lost her ring.

Compare the following:

tanam plant **Saya menanam jagung.** I plant corn.

I **Saya menanami ladang.** I plant the field.

II **Saya menanamkan jagung untuk ibu saya.** I plant corn for my mother.

Exercise 12

Add the combination **me+kan** *or* **me+i** *to the words in parentheses*

[1] Jangan (lémpar) kolam ini dengan batu. [2] Ia pandai (main) piano. [3] Siapa yang (temu) pénamu yang hilang? [4] Meréka tidak mau (dengar) naséhat orang-tua meréka. [5] Agus, pakaianmu kotor. Jangan (tidur) ranjang saya. [6] Anak kaya itu (hambur) uang ayahnya. [7] Maukah kamu (kulit) buku saya? [8] Pemburu itu (lémpar) lembing. [9] Ia (kepala) kawanan perampok. [10] Kapan Tuan Johnson (jual) mobilmu? [11] Lebih tiga tahun ia (tempat) jabatan yang penting itu. [12] Saya (pinjam) pompa kepada tetangga saya. [13] Perantau itu (rindu) tanah-airnya. [14] Diréktur penerbitan 'Daya' (tandatangan) perjanjian itu.

ENGLISH VERSION

[1] Do not throw stones into this pond. [2] She plays the piano very well. [3] Who has found your lost pen? [4] They do not want to listen to their parents' advice. [5] Agus, your clothes are dirty. Do not sleep in my bed. [6] The rich boy wasted his father's money. [7] Will you cover my book? [8] The hunter threw the spear. [9] He headed a gang of robbers. [10] When did Mr. Johnson sell your car? (for you). [11] He has occupied the important post for more than three years. [12] I lent the pump to my neighbour. [12] The traveller longed for his fatherland. [14] The director of 'Daya' publishing-house signed the contract.

CHAPTER 13

VERBS (Concluded)

The Combination of the Prefixes **mem+per**

Verbs formed from **memper** *are always* TRANSITIVE

1 *When the root word is a noun* **memper** *is a verbal extension of the idea implicit in the noun*

déwa god   **Meréka memperdéwa Raja Rimana.**
They worshipped King Rimana (*lit.* They regarded King Rimana as god).
isteri wife   **Pak Kamil memperisteri janda.** Pak Kamil married a widow (*lit.* made a widow his wife).

2 *When the root word is an adjective* **memper** *creates a verb of intensification. Sometimes the suffix* **-an** *is added.*

populér popular   **Kami mencoba memperpopulér-kan biduan itu.**   We tried to make the singer more popular.
panjang long   **Pekerja-pekerja memperpanjang jalan itu.**   Workers lengthened the road.

English has verbs such as 'to broaden', 'to heighten', 'to enlarge', 'to increase'. They are all prefixed **memper** in Indonesian: **memperlébar, mempertinggi, memperluas, memperbanyak.**

3 *When the root word is a numeral* **memper** *divides the object mentioned into the figure indicated by the root word. Sometimes the suffix* **-kan** *is added.*

tiga three   **Ibu mempertiga kué itu.**   Mother divided the cake into three.
lima five   **Guru menyuruh Amir memperlima bilang-an itu.**   The teacher asked Amir to divide the figure by five.

satu one **Hanya pemimpin besar saja dapat mem-
persatukan bangsa.** Only a great leader can unite the
nation.

Note: (1) Except for the last example, **memper**+numeral is
rarely used. Instead the verb **membagi,** to divide is used, e.g.
Kaptén itu membagi regunya menjadi dua rombongan.
The captain divided his continent into two groups.

'Saya tidak dapat membagi sembilan dengan empat,'
kata Léna. 'I can't divide nine by four,' said Lena.

(2) **memper** can be separated only in the imperative and the
passive, e.g. **Perpanjanglah ini!** Make it longer!
Jalan ini akan diperpanjang. This street will be lengthened.

Vocabulary

melalui	through	**pertama**	first
berbagai	several	**pembangunan**	building
berita	news		(present part)
baik	good	**lembaga**	institute
semua	all	**jam duabelas**	twelve o'clock
musuh	enemy	**satu jam**	one hour
bénténg	fortress	**pasukan**	troops
lukisan	painting	**jéndral**	general
jangan	do not	**pertahanan**	defence
asin	salty	**orang-bawahan**	subordinate
tawon	bee	**pencuri**	burglar, thief
madu	honey	**atap**	roof
bunga	flower	**amat**	very
di tepi	at the bank	**tua**	old
waktu	when, while	**lucu**	funny
sungai	river	**karena**	because
sesuatu	something	**tilgram**	telegram
kota	town	**bungkusan**	parcel
pembesar	authority	**tahun**	year
batu	stone	**matahari**	sun
ikan	fish	**di luar negeri**	abroad

Exercise 13

Insert the following verbs into the blank spaces below

menggembirakan to please
memanggil to call, to send for
bersekolah to go to school
mengeringkan to dry
memukul to beat
mengalami to experience
berumur to be (years) old
mengisap to suck
bermain to play
memasuki to enter
membandingkan to
  compare

berhenti to stop
memperkokoh to
  strengthen
menerima to receive, to
  get
memberikan to give
menggarami to salt
mengalir to flow
meletakkan to put
memperbudak to enslave
menyerang to attack
bersinar to shine

[1] Berita baik itu.... kita semua. [2] Musuh telah.... bénténg
kami. [3] Jangan.... lukisan saya dengan punyamu. [4] Tawon
.... madu dari bunga-bunga. [5] Waktu kami.... di tepi sungai
itu, kami.... sesuatu yang lucu. [6] Pembesar itu telah.... batu
pertama untuk pembangunan institut itu. [7] Jam duabelas kita
.... bekerja dan.... satu jam. [8] Pasukan Jéndral Ali.... perta-
hanannya. [9] Ia.... orang-bawahannya. [10] Pencuri telah....
rumah itu dari atap. [11] Pak Tirto amat tua. Ia.... sembilanpuluh tahun. [12] Sungai Brantas.... melalui berbagai kota. [13]
Ibu tak dapat.... ikan asin itu, karena matahari tidak.... [14]
Saya.... tilgram dari teman saya di Bandjarmasin. [15] Adiknya
.... di luar negeri. [16] Lestari.... gulai itu. [17] Siapa telah....
bungkusan itu kepada Tuan Harold? [18] Dapatkah Nyonya....
ténis? [19] Sudahkah kamu.... dokter? [20] Orang itu....
anaknya.

CHAPTER 14

THE PASSIVE SENTENCE

The Prefix **di-**

di+root word (with or without suffix) is equivalent to the English 'be'+past participle, e.g. **ditendang,** be kicked; **ditémbak,** be shot; **dipukuli,** be repeatedly beaten.

The passive **di-**+*root word* is used when the agent, i.e. the doer of the action, is a noun, a proper name, or the third personal pronoun singular (**ia**), or when it is not mentioned. **ia** as agent is **-nya**. It is always attached to the preposition **oléh** (by). Sometimes **oléh** is omitted. In this case **-nya** is attached to the verb.

Active:
    Dokter memeriksa saya.   The doctor examined me.
Passive:
    Saya *diperiksa* oléh dokter.   I was examined by the doctor.

Active:
    Tino menulis surat itu.   Tino wrote the letter.
Passive:
    Surat itu *ditulis* oléh Tino.   The letter was written by Tino.

Active:
    Ia menjual kuda itu.   He sold the horse.
Passive:
    Kuda itu *dijual* oléhnya, or   The horse was sold by him.
    Kuda itu *dijualnya.*

Active:
    Saya membaca pengumuman itu
Passive:
    Pengumuman itu *saya baca.*   The announcement was read
                          by me.
NEVER: **Pengumuman itu dibaca oléh saya.**

Active:
    Kamu mencurigai orang itu.   You suspected that man.

Passive:
Orang itu *kamu curigai*, or   That man was suspected by
Orang itu *kaucurigai*.   you.
NEVER: **Orang itu dicurigai oléh kamu.**

Active:
Kami mencontoh   We copied her work.
pekerjaannya.
Passive:
Pekerjaannya *kami contoh*.   Her work was copied by us.
NEVER: **Pekerjaanya dicontoh oléh kami.**

Active:
Meréka mendorong keréta   They pushed the cart.
itu.
Passive:
Keréta itu *meréka dorong*.   The cart was pushed by them.
NEVER: **Keréta itu didorong oléh meréka.**

The following sentences have two passive forms. Notice the suffix
-kan of the verbs that are followed by the preposition **kepada**
(to).

Active:
Ia menawari saya   He offered me a job.
pekerjaan.
Passive:
Saya ditawari pekerjaan   I was offered a job (by him).
(oléhnya).
Pekerjaan ditawarkan   A job was offered to me.
kepada saya (oléhnya).

Active:
Meréka memberi Kusin   They gave Kusin a gift.
hadiah.
Passive:
Kusin meréka beri hadiah.   Kusin was given a gift (by
    them).

Hadiah meréka beri*kan*   A gift was given to Kusin (by
kepada Kusin.   them).

Active:

| **Kita menyediakan tempat untuk ketua.** | We reserved a seat for the chairman. |

Passive:

| **Tempat kita sediakan untuk ketua.** | A seat was reserved for the chairman (by us). |
| **Ketua kita sediakan tempat.** | The chairman was reserved a seat (by us). |

The combination of the prefixes **di-** and **per-** is the passive of the combination **mem** and **per.**

Ia diperbudak.	He was enslaved (*lit.* He was regarded as a slave).
Jalan itu sedang diperlébar.	The road is being widened.
Meréka dipersatukan.	They were united.

The combination of the prefix **di-** and the suffix **-i** is the passive of the combination **me-** and **-i.**

Lembu itu dicambuki.	The ox was whipped (repeatedly).
Kota itu telah diduduki musuh.	The town has been occupied by the enemy.
Ikan itu dibului (disisiki).	The fish was scaled.

The combination of the prefix **di-** and the suffix **-kan** is the passive of the combination **me-** and **-kan.**

Ia ditertawakan.	He was laughed at.
Meriam ditémbakkan.	A cannon was fired.
Bendéra dikibarkan.	The flag was hoisted.

Note: The agent and the predicate of a passive sentence cannot be separated from each other. An auxiliary must be put before the agent and never between the agent and the predicate. An adverb is put at the beginning or at the end of the passive sentence.

Compare the following, noticing the place of the emphasized words:

ACTIVE: **Saya *kemarin* menemani Julia ke setasiun.** I accompanied Julia to the station yesterday.
Saya *akan* menemani Julia ke setasiun. I shall accompany Julia to the station.
PASSIVE: **Julia akan** saya temani **ke setasiun *kemarin.***
NEVER: **Saya akan** temani **Julia ke setasiun.**

Note: Sub-clauses such as in the following sentences are rendered in the passive voice in Indonesian.

Buku *yang dibeli oléhnya* mahal. The book he bought (that was bought by him) is expensive.

Meja *yang dibuat oleh ayah* di kamar. The table father made (that was made by father) is in the room.

Bunga *yang dipetik oleh Siti* berbau harum. The flower Siti picked (that was picked by Siti) smells sweet.

Dasi *yang saya pakai* dari Jepang. The tie I am wearing (that is being worn by me) is from Japan.

Suratkabar *yang kami baca* Bintang Timur. The newspaper we read (that is read by us) is Bintang Timur.

Dokter *yang mereka panggil* tinggal di Jalan Sari. The doctor they called (that was called by them) lives in Sari Street.

Exercise 14

With the help of the translation below put the following sentences into the passive voice. The root words are indicated in parentheses.

[1] Ia menyanyikan lagu merdu. [2] Meréka menerima usul Pak Diro. [3] Orang memuji keberaniannya. [4] Kami akan menolong orang miskin itu. [5] Polisi telah menyelidiki perkara itu. [6] Ia belum mengembalikan obéng saya. [7] Kamu menerbitkan buku itu. [8] Ia mendirikan rumah untuk anak-anak piatu itu (two passives). [9] Saya memperkecil belanja saya. [10] Kami menyembunyikan hadiah itu di bawah lemari. [11] Jam empat soré orang membunyikan peluit paberik (omit the agent). [12] Penonton membanjiri gedung bioskop baru itu. [13] Saya tadi melihat tas Nyonya di méja itu. [14] Orang telah menipu pedagang itu.

TRANSLATION

[1] She sang a nice song (*nyanyi*). [2] They accepted Pak Diro's proposàl (*terima*). [3] People praise his courage (*puyi*). [4] We will help the poor man (*tolong*). [5] The police have investigated the case (*selidik*). [6] He has not returned my screwdriver yet (*kembali*). [7] You publish that book (*terbit*). [8] He built a house for the orphans (*diri*). [9] I cut down my expenditure (*kecil*). [10] We hid the present under the cupboard (*sembunyi*). [11] At four o'clock in the afternoon people sound the siren of the factory (*bunji*). [12] Spectators filled the new cinema to overflowing (*banjir*). [13] I have just seen your bag lying on that table (*lihat*). [14] People have cheated the merchant (*tipu*).

Note: The Indonesian words in parentheses are root words.

CHAPTER 15

NOUNS

1 *Masculine and Feminine*
2 *Conversion*

Like their English equivalents Indonesian proper names are capitalized, e.g.

Gunung Kawi Mount Kawi; **sungai Musi** the river Musi; **Hotél Agung, Akhmad, Siti.**

In familiar Indonesian, boys' and girls' names are preceded by **si**, e.g. **si Polan, si Didi, si Tuti.** Likewise names of animals in fables are preceded by **si** or **sang**: **si Kancil** (cf. Brother Mousedeer), **sang Harimau** (cf. King Tiger).

Names of countries become names of their respective nations when they are preceded by **bangsa** and become names of their respective people when they are preceded by **orang.**

Inggeris England →**bangsa Inggeris** the English. **Orang Inggeris** Englishman.

Jérman Germany →**bangsa Jérman** the Germans. **Orang Jérman** German.

Belanda Holland →**bangsa Belanda** the Dutch. **Orang Belanda** Dutchman.

Perancis France →**bangsa Perancis** the French. **Orang Perancis** Frenchman.

Spanyol Spain →**bangsa Spanyol** the Spaniards. **Orang Spanyol** Spaniard.

Jepang Japan →**bangsa Jepang** the Japanese. **Orang Jepang** Japanese.

Filipina the Philippines →**bangsa Filipina** the Filipinos. **Orang Filipina** Filipino.

Cina China, but: **bangsa Cina** the Chinese. **Orang Cina** Chinese.

Note: Often the word **negara** (land) precedes the names of countries.

Negara Inggeris England; **Negara Arab** Arabia; **Negara Dénmark** Denmark.

English has a great number of masculine and feminine nouns. In Indonesian there are only a few of them.

MASCULINE		FEMININE	
ayah	father	**ibu**	mother
paman	uncle	**bibi**	aunt
kakék	grandfather	**nénék**	grandmother
suami	husband	**isteri**	wife
mahasiswa	boy student	**mahasiswi**	girl student
déwa	god	**déwi**	goddess
pemuda	young man	**pemudi**	girl
putera	son	**puteri**	daughter
seniman	artist	**seniwati**	woman artist
biduan	singer	**biduanita**	lady singer
raja	king	**ratu**	queen
tuan-rumah	host	**nyonya-rumah**	hostess

Other masculine nouns are indicated by **laki-laki** or **lelaki** put after them and for feminine nouns **perempuan** is used. For names of animals **jantan** and **betina** are used respectively.

orang laki-laki man		**orang perempuan** woman	
anak laki-laki boy		**anak perempuan** girl	
adik laki-laki younger brother		**adik perempuan** younger sister	
kakak laki-laki elder brother		**kakak perempuan** elder sister	
kemenakan laki-laki nephew		**kemenakan perempuan** niece	
guru laki-laki man teacher		**guru perempuan** lady teacher	
mempelai laki-laki bridegroom		**mempelai perempuan** bride	
teman laki-laki boy friend		**teman perempuan** girl friend	
kuda jantan stallion		**kuda betina** mare	
singa jantan lion		**singa betina** lioness	
sapi jantan bull		**sapi betina** cow	
harimau jantan tiger		**harimau betina** tigress	

Note: The word **'orang'** is used to refer to **people, persons** and **men**: e.g. **orang berkata**, people say; **orang gila**, a mad person, or a mad man. Often **laki-laki** is used with the omission of **orang** to refer to men: e.g. **Laki-laki mana?**, Which man?; **laki-laki itu**, that man. Similarly **perempuan** is more often used than **orang perempuan**. **Anak** refers to children, boys and girls. When it is understood that boys are meant in the conversation **anak** is used, e.g. **Anak-anak sekolah menengah putera 'ADIL'**. The boys of the 'ADIL' boys' college. Only when the sex of the young person is not understood **laki-laki** is added to **anak**, e.g. **Yang menang pertandingan itu anak laki-laki berumur 16 tahun**. It was a boy of 16 who won the match. Similarly used are **anak** and **anak perempuan**.

Conversion

Verb-roots and adjectives may be used as nouns provided they are put before possessives.

Examples:

Jalan anak itu cepat	The boy walks fast. (*Lit.* The boy's walk is fast.)
Cakapnya kasar	He talks roughly. (His talk is rough.)
Berat orang itu 80 kilogram	That man weighs 80 kilogram. (That man's weight is 80 kilogram.)
Dalam danau ini kira-kira 100 méter.	This lake is about 100 metres deep. (The depth of this lake is about 100 metres.)

Very often a verb-root or an adjective is used as a noun by adding **nya** to it. The construction of sentences with this kind of noun is illustrated in the following examples:

Tiang itu tingginya 25 méter.	That pole is 25 metres high. (*lit.* That pole, its heights is 25 metres.)
Kuda itu larinya cepat.	That horse runs fast. (*lit.* That horse, its run is fast.)

Keluarga itu hidupnya melarat.	That family lives in poverty. (*lit*. That family, its living is wretched.)

The construction above is only possible when the subject of the sentence is a noun. It is therefore wrong to say (with the intended meaning of 'he, his whispers is not audible'): **Ia bisiknya tak terdengar.** This sentence, the subject of which is a pronoun, should read:

Bisiknya tak terdengar.	His whisper was not audible.

Likewise:

Tidur saya nyenyak semalam.	I slept soundly last night.
Bacamu kurang jelas.	Your reading was not clear enough.

Not every verb-root or adjective may be used as a noun. Those that can be turned into nouns by adding affixes to them (see next chapter), e.g. **tulisan**, writing, may never be used alone as nouns without the affix. So, your writing is **tulisanmu** not **tulismu**. Likewise: our sight is **penglihatan kita** not **lihat kita**.

her beauty is **kecantikannya** not **cantiknya**.

Exercise 15

Change the following in such a way that the italicised words become nouns. Use 2 forms where possible.

Examples: Tukang itu *bekerja* amat rajin.
Kerja tukang itu amat rajin.
Tukang itu kerjanya amat rajin.

[1] Anak ini *menangis* amat keras. [2] Meriam itu *berbunyi* dahsyat. [3] Ia *menjawab* dengan senyum. [4] Kakak Mira *menyanyi* amat merdu. [5] Saya sekarang *berumur* 40 tahun. [6] Jembatan ini *panjang* (200 méter). [7] Beras sekarung ini *berat* (50 kilogram). [8] Meréka *mengira* bahwa kita bersaudara. [9] Ia *memikir* bahwa soal itu dapat dipecahkan dengan gampang. [10] Kulit ini *tebal* (0.5 séntiméter). [11] Rambutnya *berwarna* coklat. [12] Anjing si Dodi *menggonggong* keras sekali. [13] Lilin ini *menyala* amat terang. [14] Taman ini *luas* (100 héktar).

ENGLISH VERSION

[1] This child cries very loud. [2] The cannon sounded tremendously. [3] She answered with a smile. [4] Mira's sister sings very sweetly. [5] I am now 40 years old. [6] This bridge is 200 metres long. [7] This sack of rice weighs 50 kilograms. [8] They thought that we were brothers. [9] He thought that the problem could be easily solved. [10] The leather is 0·5 centimetres thick. [11] Her hair is brown. [12] Dodi's dog barks very loudly. [13] This candle burns very brightly. [14] This park is 100 hectares wide.

CHAPTER 16

NOUNS (Continued)

1 *The Prefix* **pe-**
2 *Suffix* **-an**
3 *The Combinations* **pe+an, per+an, ke+an**
4 *The Suffixes* **-man, -wan, -wati**

Many nouns are formed by adding affixes to verb-roots and adjectives. The prefix **pe-** brings about the same consonantal changes to the root word as the prefix **me-**.

1 *When the root word is a verb* **pe-** *denotes:*

   (*a*) the performer of the action

lari	run	**pelari**	runner
curi	steal	**pencuri**	thief
tulis	write	**penulis**	writer

   (*b*) the means by which the action is performed (in this case the root word may also be a noun)

suruh	order	**pesuruh**[1]	errand boy
hapus	erase	**penghapus**	eraser
garis	line	**penggaris**	ruler

2 *When the root word is a noun* **pe-** *denotes:*
the person that works or lives at the place indicated in the root word

rimba	forest	**perimba**	forester
laut	sea	**pelaut**	seaman
gunung	mountain	**penggunung**	mountaineer

3 *When the root word is an adjective* **pe-** *denotes:*
   (*a*) a person having the quality indicated in the root word (sometimes it is the abstract quality that is indicated)

[1] The initial 's' does not make the 'pe' become 'peny' in this word to distinguish it from 'penyuruh'—the one who gives orders. But 'selidik' —to search, 'penyelidik'—investigator.

malas	lazy	**pemalas**	lazybones
marah	angry	**pemarah**	bad-tempered person
besar	great	**pembesar**	authority

(b) thing that causes a person or another thing to have the quality indicated in the root word

sakit	sick	**penyakit**	disease
rusak	out of order	**perusak**	destructive agent, destroyer
manis	sweet, pretty	**pemanis**	ornament, any object that beautifies a person or thing.

The Combination pe+an

Nouns with the prefix **pe-** and the suffix **-an** are mostly abstract nouns or nouns indicating place:

layar	sail	**pelayaran**	navigation
temu	find	**penemuan**	find, invention
kubur	bury	**pekuburan**[1]	cemetery
terbit	appear	**penerbitan**	publishing company

The combination **per+an** is used instead of **pe+an** when it is derived from a word prefixed **ber-**

berjalan	to walk	**perjalanan**	journey
berkumpul	to gather	**perkumpulan**	gathering
bersembunyi	to hide	**persembunyian**	hiding-place

The Suffix -an

A great number of nouns is formed by adding **-an** to the root word.

Nouns with the suffix **-an** *denote:*

(a) the result of the action indicated in the root word:

| **hukum** | punish, sentence | **hukuman** | punishment, sentence |

[1] The initial 'k' does not make the 'pe' become 'peng' in this word to distinguish it from 'penguburan'—burial.

lukis	paint	**lukisan**	picture, painting
ajar	teach	**ajaran**	teaching

(*b*) place that is related to the basic idea indicated in the root word:

kurung	imprison, enclose	**kurungan**	prison, cage
lingkung	surround	**lingkungan**	surroundings
kubur	bury	**kuburan**	grave

(*c*) thing or tool used for the action indicated in the root word:

ayun	swing	**ayunan**	swing
timbang	weigh	**timbangan**	scales
ukur	measure	**ukuran**	measurement

(*d*) object of the action indicated in the root word:

hidang	serve	**hidangan**	dishes, comestibles
pakai	use, wear	**pakaian**	clothes
makan	eat	**makanan**	eatables

(*e*) collective noun derived from the one indicated in the root word (with or without reduplication of the root word)

buah	fruit	**buah-buahan**	fruits
sayur	vegetable	**sayuran**	vegetables
kotor (adj.)	dirty	**kotoran**	dirt, refuse

The Prefix **ke-** and the Combination **ke+an**

There are only three nouns with the prefix **ke-**, viz. **ketua**, chairman (root word **tua**, old), **kehendak**, wish (root word **hendak**, wish) and **kekasih**, lover (root word **kasih**, love).

Notice that **ke-** does not bring any consonantal change to the root word.

The Combination **ke+an** *makes:*

(*a*) abstract nouns:

bodoh	stupid	**kebodohan**	stupidity
buruk	bad	**keburukan**	badness, wickedness
curang	dishonest	**kecurangan**	dishonesty

(b) nouns indicating places:

diam	stay	**kediaman**	residence
bupati	regent	**kebupatian**	regency
raja	king	**kerajaan**	kingdom

The Suffix -man, -wan, -wati

The last of this series of affixed nouns are those which have the suffixes **-man**, **-wan**, **-wati**. They mostly denote persons having the quality indicated in the root word. This kind of noun has become popular and a few have been added to this class quite recently. **-man** and **-wan** are used for masculines and **-wati** for feminines.

However, they cannot be compared to the English suffixes **-or**, **-ess** as in 'actor', 'actress', because in Indonesian, not every masculine noun has its feminine equivalent.

bangsa	standing	**bangsawan**	nobleman
budi	benefaction	**budiman**	benefactor
harta	wealth	**hartawan**	wealthy man
seni	art	**seniman**	artist
		seniwati	woman artist
guna	use	**gunawan**	worthy citizen, philanthropist
usaha	enterprise	**usahawan**	business executive
karya	creation	**karyawan**	creator
olahraga	sport	**olahragawan**	sportsman
		olahragawati	sportswoman
negara	state	**negarawan**	statesman
warta	news	**wartawan**	reporter
peraga	showy person	**peragawati**	mannequin

Coming to the end of this chapter one might well ask whether all root words may be turned to nouns by affixing them. When is **pe-** used? When **pe+an**? When **-an**? and when **ke+an**?

A good Indonesian dictionary, or better, careful observation of the spoken or written language will be the surest guide.

The learner must accept that some irregularities are unpredictable.

Vocabulary

dipimpin to be led	**tersebut** mentioned (above mentioned)
pidato speech	
bahwa that (conjunction)	**barang tersebut** the thing mentioned
banyak many	
di antara among	**agar** (in order) that
para word used to pluralize nouns, e.g. **para hadirin,** those present; **para ibu,** mothers	**apa-apa** whatsoever
	menghalangi to obstruct, hamper
	diramaikan to be animated, to be enlivened
anggota member	
menjadi to become	**cukup** quite, enough
aktif active	**menarik** attractive
untuk to, for	**minuman** drinks
hidangan refreshments	**disajikan** to be served
disebabkan to be caused	**memakai** to wear
para undangan guests	**bergemerlapan** sparkling
memajukan to improve, to advance	**undangan** invitation

Exercise 16

Make nouns from the words in parentheses and translate the following passage:

(tua) (kumpul) 'Servias' berpidato pada (temu) itu. Ia berkata bahwa terdapat banyak (guna) di antara para anggota 'Servias', yang menjadi (bantu) aktif untuk memajukan (kumpul) tersebut. Ia mengharap agar tidak ada (halang) atau (rintang) apa-apa yang dapat menghalangi (maju) 'Servias'.

(temu) itu diramaikan oléh (tari) dan (nyanyi) yang cukup menarik. (hidang) dan (minum) disajikan pada para undangan. (usaha), (lukis), (tari) dan (peraga) hadir pada (temu) itu. Isteri para (harta) memakai (hiasan) yang bergemerlapan. (lancar) (temu) itu disebabkan karena (selenggara) dipimpin oléh (tua) sendiri, seorang (karya) pésta-pésta besar. (tutup) (temu) itu diramaikan dengan (nyanyi) bersama.

Vocabulary

artist	**lukis**	song	**nyanyi**
dancer	**tari**	business executive	**usaha**
mannequin	**peraga**	association	**kumpul**
meeting	**temu**	worthy citizen	**guna**
wealthy man	**harta**	helper	**bantu**
ornament	**hias**	hindrance	**halang**
smoothness	**lancar**	obstacle	**rintang**
arrangement	**selenggara**	progress	**maju**
chairman	**tua**	dance	**tari**
organizer (creator)	**karya**	refreshment	**hidang**
closing	**tutup**	drink	**minum**

Note: The Indonesian words are root words.

CHAPTER 17

THE IMPERATIVE

The imperative may be either a verbal root or an affixed verb. In the imperative form verbs prefixed **me-** or **ber-** retain their respective prefixes; verbs prefixed **memper-** drop their **mem** and verbs prefixed **me-** and suffixed **-kan** or **-i** drop their **me-**.

The suffix **-lah** makes the command less abrupt.

Pergi! Pergilah! Go!
Duduk! Duduklah! Sit down!
Menari! Menarilah! Dance!
Menepi! Menepilah! Move aside!
Berhenti! Berhentilah! Stop!
Berjalan! Berjalanlah! Walk!
Perbesarlah lingkaran ini! Enlarge this circle!
Lemparkanlah bola itu! Throw the ball!
Siramilah tanaman itu! Water the plants!

To make the imperative sound politer the word **silakan** or **tolong** (*lit.* help) is put before the verb. Both words are the equivalent of the English 'please'.

Silakan duduk. Sit down, please.
Silakan masuk. Come in, please.
Tolong ambilkan selop saya. Get my slippers, please.
Tolong tutupkan pintu itu. Shut the door, please.

Requests

Silakan and **tolong** cannot be used with interrogative sentences or requests. The word **sudilah** is used instead.

Will you help me, please? or Would you help me, please? is

Sudilah kamu menolong saya? (See note Chapter 6 for the use of **kamu**).

Some more examples of requests.

Sudilah Tuan menutup pintu? Would you mind closing the door?

Sudilah Nyonya meminjamkan saya lima rupiah? Could you lend me five rupiahs, please?

Sudilah Bapak berhenti sebentar? Will you stop for a moment, please?

'Let us' is translated into **mari kita** or **marilah kita.**

Let us go.	**Mari kita pergi** or merely, **Marilah.**
Let us sing.	**Marilah kita menyanyi.**
Let us take a rest.	**Mari kita beristirahat.**

Negative Imperative

The word **jangan** or **janganlah** (don't) opens a negative imperative.

Jangan lari!	Don't run!
Janganlah kamu berani!	Don't you dare!
Janganlah kita berselisih!	Don't let us quarrel!
Jangan!	Don't do it! or Stop it!

Often, the passive **di-** follows the negative **jangan.**

Jangan dipukul anak itu. Don't beat the child. (This child is not to be beaten.)

Janganlah didjual barang ini. Don't sell this thing.

Jangan dikira bahwa saya tak mengetahui hal itu. Don't think that I don't know about that matter.

When put into the active, the subject **kamu, Tuan** and other forms of the second person precede the verb.

Jangan kamu memukul anak itu. Don't (you) beat that child.

Janganlah Tuan menjual barang ini. Don't (you) sell this thing.

Jangan Saudara mengira bahwa saya tak mengetahui hal itu. Don't (you) think that I don't know about that matter.

Other Uses of **-lah**

The suffix **-lah** is also used for emphasis. It is put on the stressed word, which is mostly followed by **yang**.

Dialah yang dipanggil, bukan kamu.   It was he who was called not you.

Samunlah yang selalu membanyol.   It is Samun who is always joking.

Buku inilah yang kamu cari?   Is it this book you are looking for?

The subject mostly follows the predicate which has the suffix **-lah**. Sentences such as the following ones usually begin with an adverb.

Tiba-tiba muncullah badut itu.   Suddenly the clown appeared.

Akhirnya berkelahilah kedua anak itu.   Finally the two boys started to fight.

Maka[1] menyerahlah panglima itu.   Then the commander surrendered.

Another suffix of emphasis is **-pun**. It may be attached to any word. English uses 'too', 'even', 'ever'.

Sayapun héran.   I was surprised too.

Dudukpun ia tak dapat, apalagi berdiri.   She cannot even sit up, let alone stand up.

---

[1] **Maka** usually introduces an afterthought; it indicates a conclusion and may also introduce a new sentence. The English equivalents of it are 'then', 'after that', 'consequently'.

Maka majulah meréka.	Then they advanced.
Maka terjadilah pertempuran.	Consequently a battle broke out.

Conversation

DIKANTORPOS

Mr. Dundan. **Saya mau mengirim tilgram.**

Clerk: **Sudahkah Tuan mengisi formulir?**

D. **Inilah. Saya harap semuanya terisi dengan betul.**

C. **Ya, ini sudah betul, tetapi tulisan Tuan kurang jelas. Alamat harus Tuan tulis dengan jelas sekali.**

D. **Maafkan! Akan saya tulis sekali lagi. Betulkah ini sekarang?**

C. **Ya. Akan Tuan kirim kawat biasa atau penting?**

D. **Berapa harga kawat biasa dan berapa penting?**

C. **Harga kawat biasa lima rupiah tiap kata dan penting sepuluh rupiah.**

D. **Saya minta penting. Isi tilgram ini amat penting.**

C. **Tilgram ini berisi delapan kata. Harganya delapanpuluh rupiah.**

D. **Bilamana sialamat akan menerimanya?**

C. **Kira-kira tiga jam.**

D. **Terima kasih. Dapatkah saya membeli perangko di sini?**

C. **Tidak, di lokét sebelah.**

AT THE POST-OFFICE

D. I want to send a telegram.

C. Have you filled in the form?

D. Here it is. I hope everything is filled in all right.

C. Yes, it is all in order, but your handwriting is not clear enough. You should write the address very clearly.

D. I'm sorry. I'll write once again. Is it all right now?

C. Yes. Do you want to send it at normal or urgent rate?

D. What does an ordinary wire cost, and how much is urgent?

C. The normal rate is five rupiahs a word and urgent is ten rupiahs.

D. I want to send it urgently. The message of this telegram is very important.

C. The telegram has eight words. It will cost eighty rupiahs.

D. When will the addressee receive it?

C. In about three hours.

D. Thank you. Can I get some stamps here?

C. No, next window.

ADJECTIVES

Besides adjectival roots, e.g. **tua**, old; **muda**, young; **mudah**, easy, there are also adjectives which are formed by a verbal root and the prefix **ter-**. They correspond to the English past participle. Indonesian regards 'ter+verbal root' as an adjective since it denotes a state, e.g.

Pintu tertutup.	A closed door.
Pintu itu tertutup.	The door is closed. (cf. **pintu itu ditutup**, the door is being closed.)
Jendéla terbuka.	An open window.
Jendéla itu terbuka.	The window is open.
Penjahat itu tergantung.	The criminal was hanged.

Another affixed adjective is that with the prefix **ke-** and the suffix **-an**. Again, it is equivalent to the English past participle. Sometimes it corresponds to the English present participle or the predicative adjective.

Saya kehujanan.	I was caught in the rain.
Itu kelihatan dari sini.	It is seen from here.
Meréka kelaparan.	They were starving.
Kami kekurangan obat-obatan.	We were short of medicine

When **tidak** is put before **ter-** the English translation is also 'cannot be'.

Nyeri itu tidak tertahan.	The pain cannot be borne. (The pain is not to be borne.)
Buah ini tidak termakan.	This fruit cannot be eaten.

ter- also indicates that an action is done accidentally or without the agent's knowing.

Ia tertémbak mati.	He was accidentally killed.
Saya tertidur.	I fell asleep.
Kunci itu terbawa oléh ibu.	Mother took the key without her knowing it.
Terdengar oléh kami musik.	We heard music (*lit.* Music was heard by us without our listening to it.)

Note: The prefix **ter-** also corresponds to the English passive infinitive.

Meriam kita akan terlihat oléh musuh.	Our cannon will be seen by the enemy.
Tujuan harus tercapai.	The aim must be achieved.

Compare the difference between **ter-** and **di-**:

ter- denotes possibility or accident, e.g. **Dia tertémbak.** He is shot by accident.

di- denotes what can be seen to be done, something still not completed at the time of speaking, e.g. **Dia ditémbak.** He is shot.

Indefinite Adjectives

The following words are indefinite adjectives. They *precede* the nouns they qualify.

semua, all; **lain,** other; **keduanya,** both; **beberapa,** some; **sedikit,** little; **tiap-tiap,** each; **masing-masing,** each, every; **banyak,** many, much; **cukup,** enough, sufficient.

Semua orang harus mati.	All people must die.
Beberapa buku dirampas.	Some books were confiscated
Berilah saya sedikit cuka.	Give me a little vinegar, please.

Degrees of Comparison

The degrees of comparison are quite simple. The only rule is that the comparative and the superlative are formed by placing **lebih** and **paling** (respectively) before the positive. The superlative may also be formed by prefixing the positive with **ter-**. Sometimes **tambah** is used instead of **lebih** for the comparative.

besar, great; **lebih besar,** greater; **paling besar** or **terbesar,** greatest.

cantik, beautiful; **lebih cantik,** more beautiful; **paling cantik** or **tercantik,** most beautiful.

baik, good; **lebih baik,** better; **paling baik** or **terbaik,** best.

Ali pandai. Adiknya lebih pandai. Tetapi temannya, Jodi, paling pandai. Ali is clever. His younger brother is cleverer. But his friend, Jodi, is the cleverest.

Siapakah orang tertua di dunia? Who is the oldest man in the world?

Ia sombong, karena ia orang paling kaya di désa ini. He is proud because he is the richest man in the village.

Sri menjadi tambah gemuk.[1] Sri has put on weight.

Equality is expressed by **se-** or **sama....-nya dengan** or by **sama....-nya.**

Inequality is expressed by **tidak se-** or **tidak sama....-nya** or by **tidak sama....-nya.**

Ayah saya *setinggi* **paman saya** **Ayah saya** *sama tingginya* **dengan paman saya.**	My father is as tall as my uncle.
Ayah saya dan paman saya *sama tingginya.*	My father and my uncle are the same height.
Pérak *tidak seberat* **emas.**	Silver is not as heavy as gold.
Ia *tidak sama manisnya* **dengan kakaknya.**	She is not as pretty as her sister.
Kapas dan kapok *tidak sama beratnya.*	Cotton-wool and kapok are not the same weight.

The *comparative of superiority* is expressed by **lebih....daripada.**

Pekerjaanmu lebih baik daripada punya Omar. Your work is better than Omar's.

Kayu sawo lebih berat daripada kayu jati. Sawo-wood is heavier than jati-wood (teak).

[1] **gemuk** stout, fat.

The *comparative of graduation* is expressed by **makin,** or **semakin,** or **makin lama. . . . makin.**

Bis berjalan makin lambat.
Bis berjalan semakin lambat. } The bus drove slower and
Bis berjalan makin lama makin lambat. slower.[1]

The *comparative of proportion* is expressed by **makin. . . . makin.** The subject is usually not repeated and may be put either at the beginning or at the end of the sentence.

Ia makin tua makin tenang. } The older he grew the
Makin tua makin tenang ia. more patient he became
Makin banyak makannya makin malas ia. The more he eats the lazier he gets. (*lit.* The greater his eating, etc.)
Makin sedikit penghasilannya makin sedih ia. The less he earns the sadder he gets. (*lit.* The less his earnings, etc.)

The relative superlative that expresses the highest degree of a quality in one or more out of a greater number of persons or things is expressed by **yang.** It is put before the superlative. Often the subject is emphasized by adding the suffix **-lah** to it.

Dari murid-murid saya Saidlah yang paling rajin. Of all my pupils, Said is the most diligent.
Dialah orang terkuat dari perkumpulan olahraga kami. He is the strongest man in our sports club.

Vocabulary

anéh strange, odd	**pingsan** unconscious, to faint
banyak many	**mengangkut** to carry
bulan moon, month	**tempat** place, spot
bambu bamboo	**pertempuran** battle
bersinar to shine	**setelah** after
langit sky	**jarak** distance
terkunci locked	**jernih** clear
danau lake	**pengikut** participant
kuat strong	**terluka** wounded
berkilau-kilauan to glitter	**gerak-jalan** march

[1] English expresses this adverbially.

kehausan	thirsty	**malas**	lazy
seolah-olah	like, as if	**rotan**	rattan, cane
gemuk	thick-set, fat, stout	**kuda**	horse
cermin	mirror	**sengit**	fierce
désa	village	**selalu**	always
marah	angry	**ramah**	friendly
terjadi	happened	**membuka**	to open
hal	phenomenon, matter	**cepat**	fast
kaya	rich	**tak berawan**	cloudless
berdiri	to stand	**bagus**	fine, nice
terik	heat	**bulat**	round
matahari	sun	**rindang**	shady
dibenci	to be hated	**km**	abbreviation for kilometre
kikir	avaricious		

Exercise 18a

Fill the blank spaces with suitable adjectives from the vocabulary above.

[1] Bulan bersinar di langit yang....[2] Danau yang....itu berkilau-kilauan seolah-olah sebuah cermin....[3] Kami mendengar, bahwa di désa A terjadi hal yang....[4] Seorang gadis ....yang telah berdiri lebih dari dua jam di bawah terik matahari jatuh pingsan. [5] Teman-temannya mengangkutnya ke tempat yang....[6] Dalam pertempuran....itu....serdadu....[7] Setelah berjalan jarak dua km pengikut-pengikut gerak-jalan itu....[8] Siapa yang paling....dari guru-gurumu? [9] Mobil Tuan sama....nya dengan punya Tuan Holm. [10] Kursi....ini tidak se....kursi rotan itu. [11] Makin lama makin....lari kuda itu. [12] Si Ali makin...., ayahnya selalu....padanya. [13] Pintu ini...., saya tak dapat membukanya. [14] Orang yang.... dan....itu dibenci orang.

Exercise 18b

Find words to express the opposite meaning to the words in italics.

[1] Kami *gembira* mendengar kabar *baik* itu. [2] Sungai ini *dangkal*. [3] Orang yang *boros* itu berhutang pada sana-sini. [4] Keméja ini terlalu *sempit* untuk saya. [5] Adik si Kamil amat *pandai*. [6] Barang apa yang *teringan* di ruang ini? [7] Keluarga Jonas hidup *mewah*. [8] Pisau ini *tumpul*. Asahlah! [9] Permukaan

papan ini masih *kasar*. [10] Adik saya *tertidur*. [11] Makin *jauh* kami pergi makin *sedikit* orang yang kami jumpai. [12] Latihan ini lebih *gampang* daripada yang semula. [13] Jalan mana yang paling *ramai* di kota Pontianak? [14] Si Rusli adalah murid yang paling *malas*.

TRANSLATION

[1] We are glad to hear the good news. [2] This river is shallow. [3] That extravagant man is in debt to many people. [4] This shirt is too tight for me. [5] Kamil's younger brother is very clever. [6] What is the lightest thing in this room? [7] The Jonases live luxuriously. [8] This knife is blunt. Sharpen it! [9] The surface of this board is still rough. [10] My little sister fell asleep. [11] The farther we went the fewer people we met. [12] This exercise is easier than the last one. [13] Which is the busiest street in Pontianak? [14] Rusli is the laziest pupil.

CHAPTER 19

REDUPLICATION

Reduplication is the repetition of the root word, e.g.

Root word **anak,** child.
> *Anak-anak* **Pak Simin sangat nakal.** Mr. Simin's children are very naughty.

Root word **jalan,** walk
> **Meréka** *berjalan-jalan* **di taman yang indah.** They are walking in a lovely park.

Root word **tinggi,** high
> **Lémparkan bola ini** *setingi-tingginya,* **Ali!** Throw this ball as high as possible, Ali!

Grammatically, there are three types of duplication.

1 *Complete duplication:* the root word is repeated without any addition of a prefix, suffix, infix or change of sound.

Root word **siapa,** who
> *Siapa-siapa* **menemukan kunci yang hilang itu harus memberikannya kepada kepala-sekolah.** Whoever finds the lost key should give it to the headmaster.

Root word **barang,** thing, chattel, personal property.
> **Dia menjual** *barang-barangnya* **dengan kerugian yang besar.** He sold his goods with great loss.

Root word **mula,** start, source
> **Kedua penjudi itu** *mula-mula* **bertengkar, kemudian pukul-memukul dan akhirnya tikam-menikam.** The two gamblers first quarrelled, then they hit each other and finally they stabbed each other.

2 *Partial duplication:* a prefix, suffix or infix is added to the repeated root word.

Root word **lari,** run; **nyanyi,** sing
> **Ada yang** *berlari-lari,* **ada yang** *menyanyi-nyanyi.* Some are running about, others are singing.

Root word **kenang,** recall
> **Buku ini saya kirimkan padamu sebagai *kenang-kenangan*.** I sent you this book as a remembrance.

Root word **turun,** down
> **Penyakit itu rupanya penyakit *turun-menurun*.** That disease seems to be a hereditary one.

3 *Duplication with a change of sound:* there is a change of consonant(s) or vowel(s) in the second word. This duplication is a standing phrase. Neither of the two words is used on its own.

Root word **lauk,** complementary dish served with a rice meal
> ***Lauk-pauk* sudah dihidangkan di méja-makan.** Dishes of all sorts are already served on the dining-table.

Root word **serba,** of all sorts
> **Majalah bulanan 'Sadar' memuat *serba-serbi* karangan.** The monthly 'Sadar' contains miscellaneous articles.

huru-hara, clamour, revolt
> **Terjadi banyak *huru-hara* di negara yang baru merdéka itu.** There occur many revolts in that newly independent country.

The meaning of duplication

1 *Indefinite plurality.* Indonesian has no plural in 's'. Often the plural is simply not expressed.

Hence: I bought mangoes (or a mango). **Saya membeli mangga.** (not **mangga-mangga**).
           He sells shoes. **Ia menjual sepatu.** (not **sepatu-sepatu**).

Observe: One *usually* buys more than one mango. One sells more than one shoe.

Whereas: ***Mangga-mangga* yang dijual di pasar sangat masak.** The mangoes (all sorts of mangoes) that are sold at the market are quite ripe.

           ***Sepatu-sepatunya* belum pernah dipakainya.** His shoes (all his shoes) have never been worn.

Sometimes the indefinite plural is intensified by the suffix **-an.**

Dokter menganjurkan pada saya untuk makan *buah-buahan.* The doctor advised me to eat plenty of fruit.

Dia menanam *sayur-sayuran.* He plants vegetables of all sorts.

Compare: **Dia menanam *sayur* bukan *pohon.*** He plants a row of vegetables, not a tree.

2 With words indicating *quality, duration, state, time* and *degree* the duplication is used for the sake of *intensity* and *emphasis* on *duration,* quality of the object or mode of action.

Perhiasan-perhiasan di toko emas itu *mahal-mahal.* The ornaments at the jeweller's are extremely expensive.

Meréka berjudi *berhabis-habisan.* [1] They gambled to complete exhaustion (of funds).

If the duplicated word is accompanied by the prefix **se-** and the suffix **-nya** it indicates the highest possible degree.

Kerjakanlah *sebaik-baiknya.* Do it as well as possible.

Prajurit-prajurit kami mempertahankan bénténgnya *sekuat-kuatnya.* Our soldiers defended their fortress to the utmost (*lit.* as strongly as possible).

3 *Resemblance.* The resemblance to the real meaning of the root word is sometimes fanciful.

Anak-anak itu bermain-main *perang-perangan* di pekuburan. The children were playing a game of war at the cemetery.

Mata-mata itu tertangkap dan telah dijatuhi hukuman mati. The spy was captured and was sentenced to death.

Tukang-kayu itu mempergunakan *kuda-kuda* untuk mengetam papan itu. The carpenter uses a trestle to plane the board.

Note: **perang** war   **kuda** horse
     mata eye

---

[1] **habis** used up, out of stock.

4 Duplicated *verbs* (only the root is repeated) indicate an *indefiniteness* of *time*, *duration* or *purpose* of the *action*.

> **Meréka *tertawa-tawa* karena meréka gembira.** They were laughing (at nothing in particular) because they were happy.
>
> **Anjing gembala itu *berlari-lari* di padang rumput.** The shepherd dog was running about in the paddock.
>
> **Pelayan toko: 'Perlu pakai apa, Tuan?'** Shop assistant: 'Can I help you, Sir?'
>
> **Laki-laki: 'Saya hanya *melihat-lihat* saja.'** Man: 'I'm just having a look round.'

5 *Mutual Action.* In this case the subject must be plural. There are two forms of this duplication viz. the duplication with **ber-** and the suffix **-an,** and the reduplication with the prefix **me-** added to the second word.

> **Kedua lawan itu *berhantam-hantaman*.** The two opponents beat each other.
>
> **Meréka *bersalam-salaman*.** They shook hands.
>
> **Marilah kita *tolong-menolong*.** Let us help each other.
>
> ***Surat-menyurat* dengan orang-orang di seluruh dunia amat menarik.** Correspondence with people all over the world is quite interesting.

List of Idiomatic Words which are always used in their duplicated form

apa-apa	anything, whatever
siapa-siapa	anybody, whoever
di mana-mana	anywhere, wherever
kapan-kapan	some other time (not now, but later)
baru-baru ini	quite recently
hampir-hampir	almost
masing-masing	each
paru-paru	lungs
pertama-tama **mula-mula** }	first of all
seolah-olah **seakan-akan** }	as if, like

tiba-tiba ⎫	
sekonyong-konyong ⎭	suddenly
kira-kira	about, approximately
bersama-sama	together
sekurang-kurangnya	at least
kadang-kadang ⎫	
sekali-sekali ⎬	occasionally
sewaktu-waktu ⎭	
sekali-kali tidak	never
lebih-lebih	especially
berangsur-angsur	in instalments
moga-moga ⎫	may (used at the beginning of a prayer or a wish); **mudah-**
mudah-mudahan ⎭	**mudahan berhasil,** good luck!
anai-anai	white ant
aba-aba	command (in gymnastics, marching, etc.)
angan-angan	thought
alang-alang	reed
agar-agar	gelatin
alun-alun	town square
anting-anting	ear-ring
biri-biri	sheep
bayang-bayang	shadow
baling-baling	propeller
gara-gara	indirect cause, unexpected result
gerak-gerik	conduct, actions, doings
guna-guna	magic means
desas-desus	rumour, rumours
hujan rintik-rintik	drizzling rain
iseng-iseng	pastime
kunang-kunang	firefly
kupu-kupu	butterfly
kura-kura	tortoise
ikan lumba-lumba	porpoise
layang-layang	kite
labah-labah	spider
kanak-kanak	little child

oléh-oléh	gifts one brings home from a journey
laki-laki	man, male, masculine
langit-langit	ceiling, palate
sudut siku-siku	angle of 90 degrees
teka-teki	riddle, puzzle
undang-undang	rule, regulation
bermacam-macam **berbagai-bagai** **berjenis-jenis** **berupa-rupa** }	various
hampir-hampir tidak	hardly
sewenang-wenang	arbitrary
cuma-cuma	free of charge
tergesa-gesa **terburu-buru** }	hasty
hati-hati	careful
samar-samar	dim
compang-camping	in rags
rata-rata	average, equally
mentah-mentah	resolute
mati-matian	with great effort
luntang-lantung	idle
berlimpah-limpah **berlebih-lebih** }	abundant
bolak-balik **mondar-mandir** }	to and fro
pura-pura	for the sake of appearance
terserak-serak **kucar-kacir** **morat-marit** }	disordered
pelahan-lahan **pelan-pelan** }	slow, soft
gilang-gemilang	sparkling, dazzling
béngkak-béngkok	twisting
berliku-liku	winding
lekak-lekuk	rough (of roads)
terang-terangan	frank
ragu-ragu	doubtful

olok-olok	ridicule
gembar-gembor	to trumpet forth, blazon abroad
berduyun-duyun	to flock, go in groups
bersenang-senang	to enjoy oneself
beramai-ramai	to do something noisily or together
terombang-ambing	rising and falling (of a ship)
terengah-engah	to pant
minta-minta	to beg
terbahak-bahak	to laugh heartily
berjalan-jalan	to stroll
berulang-ulang	again and again

Exercise 19

Put the words in parentheses in their correct duplicated form.

[1] Pemilik toko itu menjual barangnya (murah). [2] (Anak) tetangga saya (main) di bawah pohon mangga. [3] (Tawanan) perang dibébaskan setelah perang berakhir. [4] Ikatlah tali ini (erat). [5] Marilah kita bermain (serdadu). [6] Gadis itu malu waktu diperkenalkan pada bakal suaminya; mukanya (mérah). [7] Lémparkan lembing itu (jauh). [8] Siapa yang (cakap) tadi? [9] Orang yang mengamuk itu (jerit) dan menémbaki (orang) yang ada di sekitarnya. [10] Kain di toko kain ini (jélék); marilah kita (lihat) di toko lain. [11] Sudah (tahun) kedua saudara itu terpisah. [12] Maka waktu meréka berjumpa, meréka (peluk). [13] Bendéra (robék) oléh kaum pemberontak. [14] Ia membuat (kucing) dari tanah liat. [15] (Penumpang) kapal-terbang itu olahragawan semuanya. [16] Kami (cari) rumah lurah pada suatu malam, tetapi tiada kami dapati.

ENGLISH VERSION

[1] The shopkeeper sells his goods very cheaply. [2] My neighbour's children were playing under the mango-tree. [3] All prisoners of war were released when the war was over. [4] Tie this cord as tightly as possible. [5] Let us play soldiers. [6] The girl was shy when she was introduced to her prospective husband; she blushed (her face turned reddish). [7] Throw the javelin as far as you can. [8] Who was talking just now? [9] The man who ran

amuck screamed (and went on screaming) and shot (and went on shooting) at the people around him. [10] The material in this drapery store is very bad, let's have a look round in another store. [11] The two sisters had been separated for years. [12] When they met they embraced each other. [13] The flag was torn in pieces by the rebels. [14] She made a cat-like figure from clay. [15] All passengers on board the airliner were sportsmen. [16] We were looking for the house of the headman of the village one night, but we could not find it.

CHAPTER 20

COMPOUNDS

1. *Compound Nouns*
2. *Compound Adjectives*
3. *Compound Verbs*

Compounds usually consist of two different elements, both of which are for the most part root words. The two elements are sometimes joined together, sometimes they are separated by a hyphen and sometimes they are written as two separate words (cf. the English compounds, seasick, night-porter, prime minister). There are few fixed rules as to when the elements are hyphenated. (See *note* 2, below.)

1 Compound Nouns

1 *The combination noun + noun*

(*a*) The elements are opposite in meaning to one another.

tua-muda	old and young (adjectival nouns)
siang-malam	night and day
ibu-bapa	father and mother

(*b*) The elements are of similar species. Compounds such as these denote a greatness of quantity, a vastness of expanse. The English version is the indefinite adjective '*all*' or the adjectives '*big*', '*vast*' put before the noun(s).

méja-kursi	all tables and chairs
sanak-saudara saya	all my relatives
hutan-rimba	a vast forest

(*c*) Either of the elements qualifies the other.

saputangan	handkerchief (*lit.* broom for the hand)
sakitgigi	toothache
matahari	sun (*lit.* eye of the day)

(*d*) The first element denotes an attribute of the second.

lenganbaju	sleeve (*lit.* arm of the blouse)
kepala-sekolah	headmaster (*lit.* head of the school)
tali-sepatu	shoe-laces

(*e*) The second element further defines, or is in apposition to, the first. (These compounds are mostly nouns denoting occupation, position, profession.)

kota Tomohon	the town of Tomohon
negara Arab	the country of Arabia
pohon papaya	pawpaw tree
tukang-kayu	carpenter (*lit.* workman for wood)
dokter-mata	occulist (*lit.* eye doctor)
tukang-pangkas[1]	barber

2 *The combination noun + adjective*

The second element qualifies the first, often figuratively. There must always be a hyphen between the elements or the adjective would have a literal meaning.

orang-tua	parent (cf. **orang tua;** old man)
raja-muda	viceroy (cf. **raja muda,** young king)
anak-emas	favourite child, pupil etc. (cf. **cincin emas,** gold ring)

3 *The combination noun + verb-root*

The second element denotes the use or purpose of the first.

kertas-tulis	writing paper
kamar-makan	dining-room
kuda-balap	race-horse

Note: When hyphenated compound nouns need to be duplicated both elements are repeated. Thus: **kamar-makan kamar-makan.** But when there is no hyphen, **pohon-pohon mangga.**

[1] or **tukang-potong-rambut.**

2 Compound Adjectives

1 *The combination adjective + adjective*

  (a) Both elements have the same meaning and put together form an intensifying adjective. English may sometimes use such pairs or put adverbs of intensity like 'extremely', 'terribly', 'awfully', 'most' before the adjective.

lemah-lembut	sweet and gentle
indah-permai	extremely beautiful
hancur-lebur	completely destroyed.

  (b) The second element qualifies the first

mérah-tua	dark red
biru-lebam	black and blue
hijau-muda	light green

2 *The combination adjective + noun*

The first element qualifies the second in a figurative sense. It corresponds exactly to its English equivalent.

keraskepala	pigheaded, obstinate, stubborn
mukadua	two-faced
panjangtangan	light-fingered (cf. **tangan panjang**, long arm)

3 Compound Verbs

  (a) The prefix of a compound verb is attached to the first element.

membábi-buta	to act blindly
bermain-mata	to make eyes
mengadu-domba	to play people off against one another
berterima-kasih	to thank

  (b) The prefix of a compound verb is attached to the first element and the suffix to the second.

menghancur-leburkan	to destroy completely
menyatu-padukan	to unite

Vocabulary

menyuruh	to order, to command	**majemuk**	compound
kata	word	**biasanya**	usually
		jam-jam yang ramai	rush hours

Amérika Serikat U.S.A.	**masih** still
bertamasya to make an excursion	**pembunuh** murderer
kebakaran fire	**menyampaikan** to hand (something to somebody)
petani farmer	**menghidangkan** to serve[1]
pemenang winner	**lezat** delicious
perjalanan journey	**mencari nafkah** to earn a living
pusat-kota centre of the city	
kasih pada to love	**sering** often
lagipula moreover	**antara** between

Exercise 20

Put the following compounds in the blank spaces below:

pulang-pergi, to and fro; **menaruh hati,** fall in love; **ibukota,** capital city; **duta-besar,** ambassador; **besarkepala,** proud; **papantulis,** blackboard; **membanting-tulang,** toil; **lalulintas,** traffic; **cantik-juita,** very beautiful; **angkatan udara,** air force; **pasar-malam,** fair; **kaya-miskin,** rich and poor; **rumah-makan,** restaurant; **muda-belia,** very young; **mengucapkan selamat,** congratulate; **surat kepercayaan,** credentials; **perlombaan-lari,** race; **hari-libur,** holiday; **membalas dendam,** revenge oneself; **baik-hati,** good-hearted.

[1] Pak Guru menyuruh si Udong pergi ke....untuk menulis kata 'Majemuk'. [2] Pada jam-jam yang ramai banyak....di-pusat-kota. [3]....kasih pada dokter yang....itu. [4] Rustini adalah gadis yang...., lagipula ia masih....[5] Banyak pemuda ....padanya. [6] Kartono....pada pembunuh ayahnya. [7] Apakah....Amérika Serikat? [8] Bésok...., kami akan berta-masya ke Selékta. [9] Terjadi kebakaran yang besar di....itu. [10]....Inggeris yang baru sudah menyampaikan....nya kepada Présiden. [11]....mana menghidangkan makanan yang lezat itu? [12] Petani itu....untuk mencari nafkah. [13] Negara itu mem-punyai....yang kuat. [14] Kami....pada pemenang....itu. [15] Ia sering membuat perjalanan....antara Bandung dan Jakarta. [16] Orang yang....tidak mempunyai banyak teman.

[1] By Indonesian custom, the servant hands tea to the hostess who serves the guests.

CHAPTER 21

ADVERBS AND ADVERBIAL PHRASES

Adverbial phrases such as **minggu depan** (next week), **di London** (in London), **dalam tahun** 1948 (in the year 1948) are placed at the beginning or at the end of the sentence.

Examples:

Minggu depan **kakaknya akan pulang.**	Her brother will
Kakaknya akan pulang *minggu depan.*	come home next week.
Saya melihat kakakmu *di muka kantorpos.*	I saw your brother in
Di muka kantorpos **saya melihat kakakmu.**	front of the post-office.
Sejak tahun 1951 **kami tinggal di sini.**	We have lived
Kami tinggal di sini *sejak tahun 1951.*	here since 1951.

Adverbs and adverbial phrases of indefinite time are placed after the subject of the sentence or at the beginning of the sentence. They are:

selalu	always	**tiba-tiba,**	suddenly
sering	often	**sekonyong-**	
sewaktu-waktu	occasionally	**konyong**	
pernah	ever	**baru**	just
tak pernah	never	**tadi**	just now
pada umumnya	generally	**sudah, telah**	already
jarang	rarely	**sebentar**[1]	in (for) a
serentak	at once		moment
		sebentar lagi	shortly
		baru-baru ini	recently
		belakangan ini	lately
		dengan segera	immediately

---

[1] **'Tunggu sebentar!'** 'Wait a moment!'

Examples:

Pak Alim *selalu* **kekurangan uang.**   Pak Alim is always
Selalu **Pak Alim kekurangan uang.**   short of money.
Saya *sering* **berjumpa dengan Umar.** ⎱ I often meet
Sering **saya berjumpa dengan Umar.** ⎰ Umar.
Meréka *serentak* **pulang.** ⎱
Serentak **meréka pulang.** ⎰ They went home immediately.

Note: (1) When **sudah** or **telah** opens the sentence the subject is usually put at the end of the sentence, e.g.

Saya sudah melihat film itu. ⎱ I have already seen that
Sudah **melihat film itu** *saya.* ⎰ film.
Dia telah dibunuh. ⎱
Telah *dibunuh* **dia.** ⎰ He has (already) been murdered.

(2) **sebentar, sebentar lagi, baru-baru ini, belakangan ini, dengan segera** may also be placed at the end of the sentence, e.g.

Ibu ke luar *sebentar.*   Mother is out for a moment.
Ayah akan kembali *sebentar lagi.*   Father will be back shortly.
Kami mengerjakannya *dengan segera.*   We did it immediately.

Adverbs that express the degree of reality belonging to a statement are:

pasti, tentu	certainly
sebenarnya	actually
tampaknya, rupanya	apparently
mungkin	possibly
barangkali	probably
sungguh	really

They are put either after the subject of the sentence or at the beginning of the sentence.
Examples:

Regu kita *pasti* **menang.**   Our team will certainly win.
Tampaknya **kamu lelah.**   You seem to be tired.
Pelatih itu *sungguh* **kecéwa.**   The trainer was really disappointed.

Adverbs and adverbial phrases of degree are:

hampir or **hampir-hampir**	**hanya** only
nearly, almost	**seluruhnya, semuanya**
agak rather	completely
hampir-hampir tidak	**sangat, amat, sekali** very
hardly	**terlalu** too
luar biasa, bukan main	
extremely	

They are most frequently placed before the word they define.

Sekarang *hampir* **jam sebelas.** It is nearly eleven o'clock now.

Saya *hanya* **mau meminjam tangmu.** I only want to borrow your tongs.

Kami *hampir-hampir tidak* **dapat percaya.** We could hardly believe it.

Note: 1 **seluruhnya, semuanya, sangat, amat** may also be placed after the word they qualify, e:g.

Gedung itu hancur *seluruhnya.* The building was completely destroyed.

Anak laki-laki itu nakal *sangat.* That boy is very naughty.

2 **sekali** is always placed after the word it qualifies, e.g.

Ia bodoh *sekali.* He is very stupid.

Cincin ini mahal *sekali.* This ring is very expensive.

3 An emphatic **-nya** is always attached to the word that follows **bukan main** and **luar biasa,** e.g.

Balu bukan main malas*nya.* Balu is extremely lazy.

Peti ini luar biasa berat*nya.* This case is extremely heavy.

4 **hampir-hampir tidak** may be separated when placed at the beginning of the sentence, e.g.

Hampir-hampir **saya** *tidak* **dapat berjalan.** I could hardly walk.

Adverbial phrases of manner are formed mostly from adjectives preceded by **dengan** or from verbs preceded by **dengan** or **sambil.** They are usually placed after the word they qualify.

Examples:

Anak-anak itu menyanyi *dengan* **gembira.** The children sang happily (with happiness).

Rina menyapa saya *sambil* **tersenyum.** Rina greeted me smilingly (while smiling).

Ia menerangkannya *sambil* **tertawa.** He explained it laughingly (while laughing).

Most adjectives may be used as adverbs without the additional **dengan.** They precede the word they qualify. However, they may cause ambiguity to the sentence.

Take, for instance, the sentence:

Babu baru datang.

As the sentence stands it has two meanings, viz. The servant has just come, and The new servant came.

This ambiguity can be solved by means of **itu.** When **itu** is placed before **baru** it makes the latter qualify **datang.** When **baru** is followed by **itu** it becomes an adjective that qualifies **babu.**

Thus:

Babu itu *baru datang.* The servant has just come.
Babu baru **itu datang.** The new servant came.

Other examples:

Kota itu *lama diduduki* **oléh musuh.** The town was occupied by the enemy for a long time.
Kota lama **itu diduduki oléh musuh.** The old town was occupied by the enemy.
Bénsin itu *gampang terbakar.* Benzine burns easily.
Soal gampang **itu sukar bagi murid bodoh itu.** The easy sum is difficult for the stupid student.

In speech, a slight break may indicate whether an adjective qualifies a noun or whether it is an adverb, e.g.

Rumah kos : sukar didapat sekarang (pronounced with a slight break before **sukar**). Board is difficult to get nowadays.

Soal-soal sukar: **terdapat di dalam buku ini** (pronounced with a slight break after **sukar**). Difficult sums are to be found in this book.
Pekerjaan: gampang diperoléh. Jobs are easy to get.
Pekerjaan: gampang dapat diperoléh di paberik itu. An easy job can be found in that factory.

Vocabulary

menonton film to go to the movies
pergi berbelanja to go shopping
tiap pagi, tiap-tiap pagi every morning
hadiah prize
pertama first
kontés-nyanyi singing contest
kami sekeluarga our whole family
pergi berpik-nik to go for a picnic
kadang-kadang sometimes
sedekah alms

biola violin
tamat to finish
sekolah menengah atas (S.M.A.) senior high school
sekolah menengah pertama (S.M.P.) junior high school
sekolah dasar primary school
taman kanak-kanak kindergarten
bungsu youngest (child)
pengemis beggar
sempurna perfect
danau lake

Exercise 21

Put the adverb into the right place in these sentences:

[1] Adik saya menonton film dengan teman-temannya (sering). [2] Nyonya Burns pergi berbelanja tiap-tiap pagi (biasanya). [3] Kamu tinggal di désa (pernah)? [4] Saya membaca suratkabar setelah makan-malam (selalu). [5] Meréka percaya bahwa saya mendapat hadiah pertama dalam kontés-nyanyi itu (hampir-hampir tidak). [6] Kami sekeluarga pergi berpik-nik di tepi danau Toba (kadang-kadang). [7] Guru kami kembali dari luar negeri (baru). [8] Ia tamat sekolah menengah atas (bulan yang lalu). [9] Perempuan itu mengatakannya (dengan sedih). [10] Anakmu yang bungsu nakal (sangat). [11] Siapa yang memberi sedekah pada pengemis itu (tak pernah)? [12] Ia memainkan biola (dengan sempurna).

CHAPTER 22

NUMERALS

The Indonesian system of numbering is somewhat like the English system.

0	**nol**	10	**sepuluh**	20	**duapuluh**
1	**satu**[1]	11	**sebelas**	21	**duapuluh satu**
2	**dua**	12	**duabelas**	22	**duapuluh dua**
3	**tiga**	13	**tigabelas**	23	**duapuluh tiga**
4	**empat**	14	**empatbelas**	24	**duapuluh empat**
5	**lima**	15	**limabelas**	25	**duapuluh lima**
6	**enam**	16	**enambelas**	26	**duapuluh enam**
7	**tujuh**	17	**tujuhbelas**	27	**duapuluh tujuh**
8	**delapan**	18	**delanpanbelas**	28	**duapuluh delapan**
9	**sembilan**	19	**sembilanbelas**	29	**duapuluh sembilan**

10	**sepuluh**	100	**seratus**
20	**duapuluh**	101	**seratus satu**[2]
30	**tigapuluh**	122	**seratus duapuluh dua**
40	**empatpuluh**	200	**dua ratus**
50	**limapuluh**	274	**dua ratus tujuhpuluh empat**
60	**enampuluh**	300	**tiga ratus**
70	**tujuhpuluh**	400	**empat ratus**
80	**delapanpuluh**		etc.
90	**sembilanpuluh**		

[1] **satu** in compounds is **se-**.
[2] There is no equivalent of the English conjunction 'and' in compound numbers.

209   two hundred *and* nine   **dua ratus sembilan.**

1000 **seribu**
2004 **dua ribu empat**
2056 **dua ribu limapuluh enam**
2738 **dua ribu tujuh ratus tigapuluh delapan**
3000 **tiga ribu**
4000 **empat ribu**
    etc.
1000 000 **sejuta** or **satu juta**

Observe: 'one' is **suatu** in 'one day', 'one night', etc.

pada suatu hari	one day
pada suatu ketika	on one occasion
pada suatu masa	at one time

Numeral Coefficients

In English we say 'a *sheet* of paper', 'five *loaves* of bread', 'ten *bottles* of beer'. In Indonesian there are plenty of such coefficients and they are more in use and more varied than in English.

In English we say 'two cats', 'four eggs' but in Indonesian we put coefficients before 'cats' and 'eggs'. Thus **dua** *ékor* **kucing** (*lit.* two *tails* of cats) (cf. two *head* of cattle), **empat** *butir* **telur** (*lit.* four *grains* of eggs).

'One' or 'a' is always **se-** attached to the coefficient:

one or *a* book	**sebuah buku**
one or *a* man	**seorang orang laki-laki**
five men	**lima orang laki-laki**

orang is used for human beings:
seorang orang Amérika[1]	*one* or *an* American
sepuluh orang India	ten Indians

ékor is used for animals:

seékor kera	a monkey
tujuh ékor beruang	seven bears

[1] Often, however, the second **orang** is omitted.
seorang Inggeris an Englishman.
empat orang Inggeris four Englishmen.

buah is used for large things: houses, ships, mountains and also for fruit and abstract nouns.

sebuah truk	a truck
delapan buah sekolah	eight schools
seratus buah nenas	a hundred pineapples
sebuah pikiran	a thought

batang is used for any long, cylindrical objects: cigars, trees, spears, sticks.

sebatang pipa besi	an iron pipe
dua batang bambu	two bamboos

tangkai or **kuntum** is used for flowers.

setangkai bunga mawar	a rose
tiga kuntum bunga anggrék	three orchids (three blooms of orchids)

helai is used for flat, thin objects: cloth, paper.

sehelai kertas	a sheet of paper
sebelas helai saputangan	eleven handkerchiefs

bidang is used for grounds, fields, gardens.

sebidang tanah	a piece of ground.
lima bidang sawah	five fields

biji or **butir** is used for grains, seeds and anything resembling grains or seeds: corn, pearls, diamonds, eggs.

sebutir peluru	a bullet (a round of ammunition)
sepuluh biji permata	ten precious stones

bilah is used for flat, bladed objects: knives, planks.

sebilah kapak	an axe
dua bilah pisau	two knives.

pucuk is used for sharp, pointed objects: rifles, nails.

sepucuk surat[1]	a letter
beberapa pucuk bedil	some rifles

In olden times letters were rolled up resembling gun barrels.

utas is used for long, soft objects: threads, cords.

seutas tampar	a length of rope
tiga utas pita	three pieces of ribbon

potong, kerat or **carik** is used for anything that can easily be torn, broken or cut: bread, meat.

sepotong roti	a slice of bread
sekerat daging	a cut of meat
secarik kertas	a piece of paper

Note: 'one of us' is **seorang dari kami,** 'one of the horses' is **seékor dari kuda-kuda itu.**

Notice that the coefficient is always put after the cardinal number. Number and coefficient are placed before a noun when quantity is emphasized. When the noun has the emphasis number and coefficient are placed after it, e.g.

Ia mengirim dua pucuk surat.   He sent two letters.

but: **Ibu membeli ayam seekor, jeruk 20 buah dan telur 10 butir.**   Mother bought a chicken, 20 oranges and 10 eggs.

Ordinal Numbers

The prefix **ke-** attached to a cardinal number makes it an ordinal number; the only exception being **pertama,** first.

kedua	second
kesembilan	ninth
keduapuluh	twentieth
keseratus delapan	hundred and eighth
ketiga ribu	three thousandth
etc.	

Ordinals follow nouns: **hadiah kedua,** the second prize. When they are put before the noun they become cardinal numbers again, but with a definite meaning.

Compare:

gadis ketiga	the third girl
ketiga gadis	the three girls

orang kedua the second man
kedua orang the two (or both) men

The prefix **ber-** attached to a cardinal number makes the latter an adjective or an adverb, e.g.

Kami berlima.	We were five. There were five of us.
Perampok itu berempat.	The robbers were four.

but:

Kami berbaris berlima-lima.	We marched in fives.
Meréka maju berempat-empat.	They advanced in fours.

Notice the duplication!
When a tenfold cardinal is prefixed **ber-** and duplicated, it becomes an indefinite adjective.

berpuluh-puluh murid[1]	tens of pupils
beratus-ratus serdadu	hundreds of soldiers
beribu-ribu domba	thousands of sheep
berjuta-juta bintang	millions of stars
berpuluh-puluh ribu	tens of thousands
beratus-ratus ribu	hundreds of thousands

once	**sekali**	the first time	**kali pertama**
twice	**dua kali**	the second time	**kali kedua**
three times	**tiga kali**	the third time	**kali ketiga**
	etc.		etc.
firstly	**pertama-tama**		
secondly	**kedua**		
thirdly[2]	**ketiga**		
	etc.		

[1] The suffix **-an** may also be used instead, but without duplication. **puluhan, ratusan, ribuan, jutaan, puluhan ribu, ratusan ribu.**
[2] Lastly, **akhirnya**; last, **terakhir.**

Fractions

The fraction is quite simple. The line between the denominator and the numerator is in speech **per**.

$\frac{1}{2}$ **satuperdua, seperdua, setengah** (half) or **separoh** (half).

With other numbers 'half' is always **setengah.**

$12\frac{1}{2}$ **duabelas setengah**
$\frac{1}{3}$ **satu pertiga** or **sepertiga**
$\frac{1}{4}$ **satu perempat** or **seperempat**
$\frac{1}{5}$ **satu perlima** or **seperlima**
    etc.

With other numbers **seper** (not **satuper**) is always used.

$24\frac{1}{5}$ **duapuluh empat seperlima**
$\frac{2}{7}$ **dua pertujuh** $1\frac{1}{2}$ **satu setengah**
$\frac{4}{11}$ **empat persebelas** $1\frac{1}{4}$ **satu seperempat**
$\frac{8}{41}$ **delapan perempatpuluh** $2\frac{3}{8}$ **dua tiga**
         satu   **perdelapan**
    etc.   etc.

Here are some useful phrases and derivations in connection with numbers.

satu per satu   one by one
Murid-murid masuk ke kelas satu per satu.   The pupils entered the classroom one by one.
satu-satunya   the only one
Ia adalah orang satu-satunya yang dapat dipercaya.   He was the only man that could be trusted.

satuan or **kesatuan**	unit (measurement or contingent)
persatuan	federation
satu, dua	one or two
kedua-duanya	both
ketiga-tiganya	all three

'**Yang mana yang akan Tuan beli, yang besar atau yang kecil.' 'Saya ambil kedua-duanya.'**
'Which one do you want to buy, the big one or the small one?' 'I take both.'

kembar dua	twins
kembar tiga	triplets
kembar empat	quadruplets
kembar lima	quintuplets
perempatan	crossroad
kesebelasan	football team (consisting of eleven members)

Currency

Indonesia has decimal coinage. There are notes of 1000 rupiahs, 500 rupiahs, 100 rupiahs, 50 rupiahs, 25 rupiahs, 10 rupiahs, 2.5 rupiahs and 1 rupiah.

There are coins of 50 cents, 25 cents, 10 cents and 5 cents. The rupiah is shortened into Rp. The Indonesian word for 'cent' is **sén.**

Rp.   152,— **seratus limapuluh dua rupiah.**

Rp.   7,50 **tujuh rupiah limapuluh sén** or **tujuh rupiah setengah.**

Rp.   84,75 **delapanpuluh empat rupiah tujuhpuluh lima sén.**

Rp.   9,05 **sembilan rupiah lima sén.**

Rp. 6038,— **enam ribu tigapuluh delapan rupiah.**

Rp.   0,95 **sembilanpuluh lima sén.**

Rp.   0,05 **lima sén.**

Rp.   4+Rp. 5=Rp. 9 **empat rupiah** *ditambah* **lima rupiah** *menjadi* (*sama dengan*) **sembilan rupiah.**

Rp. 10−Rp. 3=Rp. 7 **sepuluh rupiah** *dikurangi* **tiga rupiah menjadi tujuh rupiah.**

Rp. 50×2=Rp. 100 **limapuluh rupiah** *dikalikan dua* **sama dengan seratus rupiah.**

Rp. 400÷8=Rp. 50 **empat ratus rupiah** *dibagi* **delapan sama dengan limapuluh rupiah.**

Clock

In Indonesia the day is divided into:

pagi (0.4–11.00), **siang** (11.00–14.00), **soré** (14.00–16.00), **petang** (16.00–19.00), and **malam** (19.00–0.4)

Compare the differences in saying the time in Indonesian and in English.

Jam (pukul) berapa sekarang?	What time is it now?
Jam 7 pagi.	(It is) 7 o'clock in the morning.
Jam setengah *duabelas siang*.	Half past *eleven* in the *morning*.
Jam setengah *satu* siang.	Half past *twelve* in the *afternoon*.
Jam 3 *soré*.	3 o'clock in the *afternoon*.
Jam 5 *petang*.	5 o'clock in the *afternoon*.
Jam 6 *petang*.	6 o'clock in the *evening*.
Jam 9 *malam*.	9 o'clock in the *evening*.
Jam 2 *malam*.	2 o'clock in the *morning*.
Jam 8 *léwat* (lebih) *seperempat*.	a quarter past eight.
Jam 8 *kurang* seperempat.	a quarter to eight.
Jam 9 léwat (lebih) 5 menit.	5 minutes past 9.
Jam 9 kurang 5 menit.	5 minutes to 9.

Note : 10 hours   10 **jam** (not **pukul**)
in time-tables.

7.45	**tujuh empatpuluh lima**	seven forty-five.
7.30	**tujuh tigapuluh**	seven thirty
2.12	**dua duabelas**	two twelve.

Exercise 22

Say in Indonesian :

[A] 6, 10, 8, 3, 9, 7, 2, 1, 5, 4, 11, 18, 16, 13, 19, 12, 17, 14, 15, 20, 29, 48, 71, 50, 36, 69, 82, 94, 203, 872, 436, 781, 594, 7745, 87045, 912875, 2045776.

[B] $4\frac{1}{4}$, $57\frac{1}{2}$, $608\frac{3}{8}$, $752\frac{11}{80}$.

[C] $4+7=11$; $12+19=31$; $8-2=6$; $104-28=76$; $10\times3=30$; $92\times2=184$; $72\div8=9$; $405\div5=81$.

[D] Rp. 11; Rp. 74; Rp. 107,25.

[E] 7 a.m.; 8.15 p.m.; 10.45 a.m.; 3.57 p.m.; 9.30 a.m.; 12.00; 4.25 p.m.; 6 p.m.

Conversation

ABDUL BERJUMPA DENGAN TEMANNYA BAKRI	ABDUL MEETS WITH HIS FRIEND BAKRI

Abdul:

Jam berapa sekarang?

A.: What time is it now?

Bakri:

Jam sembilan léwat seperempat. Kamu tampaknya terburu-buru.

B.: It is a quarter past nine. You seem to be in a hurry.

A.: **Ya, saya akan naik keréta-api sembilan empat lima.**[1]

A.: Yes, I want to catch the nine forty-five train.

B.: **Masih ada waktu setengah jam. O ya, kapan kakakmu berangkat ke Amérika?**

B.: There is still half an hour. I say, when does your brother leave for the U.S.?

A.: **Tanggal 17 Juni.**

A.: On 17th June.

B.: **Berapa lama ia akan tinggal di Amérika?**

B.: How long will he be staying in the U.S.?

A.: **Setahun. Kemudian ia akan berkeliling Éropa selama 3 bulan.**

A.: A year. Then he'll make a trip round Europe for 3 months.

B.: **Wah, untung dia! Saya harap saya juga mendapat béasiswa seperti dia.**

B.: Oh, isn't he lucky? I wish I had got a scholarship too as he did.

A.: **Saya harus pergi sekarang. Keréta-api tidak akan menunggu saya.**

A.: I must be off now. My train won't wait for me.

B.: **Selamat jalan.**

B.: Bon Voyage.

A.: **Terima kasih.**

A.: Thank you.

[1] Colloquially **pukul** is sometimes left out in timetables.

CHAPTER 23

THE PREFIX SE-

We saw in Chapter 18 and Chapter 19 that the prefix **se-** can be the equivalent of the English adverb 'as':

Selama saya hidup.	As long as I live.
Setinggi gunung.	As high as a mountain.
Sebanyak-banyaknya.	As much as possible.
Sejauh-jauhnya.	As far as possible.

Here are the other uses of **se-**:

1 Attached to a noun it denotes a 'oneness'. It corresponds to the English 'same', 'whole'.

Kami tinggal sejalan. We live in the same street.
Umi dan saya sekelas. Umi and I are classmates.
Sedésa keluar menonton pembakaran mayat itu. The whole village came out to watch the cremation.
Sekeluarga menderita penyakit mata itu. The whole family suffer from the eye-disease.

2 Attached to a verb-root it denotes time. It is identical with the English participle denoting time.

Setiba di rumah, saya masuk ke kamar saya. Coming home, I went to my room.
Sepulang dari perjalanannya, ia jatuh sakit. Arriving home from his journey, he was taken ill.
Sesampai di tempat tujuan, kami pergi menemui kepala désa. Having arrived at our destination, we went to see the headman of the village.

3 Attached to a verb-root (with or without duplication) it also denotes 'freedom of action', e.g.

Makan sesuka hatimu. Eat to your heart's content.

Ia berkata semaunya saja. He spoke bluntly (inconsiderately).

Marilah kita mencobanya, sedapat kita. Let us try it and see what we can do.

Meréka makan sekenyang-kenyangnya. They eat to their heart's content.

Vocabulary

berbuat to do, act
sekehendak high-handedly, inconsiderately
bila if
berada to be
gedung sandiwara theatre
tempat duduk seat
menggunakan, mempergunakan to use
waktu time
nasihat advice
pembunuh murderer
hukuman mati death sentence
bungkusan package, parcel

membagi-bagi to distribute
pengungsi refugee
habis terbakar burned up
memberi selamat to congratulate
memenangkan to win (transitive)
merayakan to celebrate
ditahan to be kept in custody
melakukan to commit
kemenangan victory
penipuan forgery
menémbak to shoot
harimau tiger

Exercise 23

Translate:

[1] Sungai ini panjangnya 2 km dan lébarnya 50 m. [2] Janganlah berbuat sekehendakmu saja bila kamu berada di rumah orang. [3] Gedung sandiwara 'Jutari' mempunyai 2000 tempat duduk; gedung itu gedung terbesar di kota P. [4] 'Pergunakanlah waktumu sebaik-baiknya' adalah nasihat yang sering saya terima dari ayah saya. [5] Ketiga pembunuh itu dijatuhi hukuman mati. [6] Berpuluh ribu bungkusan makanan dibagi-bagikan kepada para pengungsi itu. [7] Separoh dari hutan itu habis terbakar. [8] Meréka berbaris bertiga-tiga memasuki lapangan. [9] Pertama-tama saya akan memberi selamat pada Kasino yang memenangkan hadiah pertama. [10] Sekota mengibarkan bendéra untuk merayakan kemenangan itu. [11] Kedua saudara itu ditahan karena meréka telah melakukan penipuan. [12] Tuan Smith telah menémbak tiga ékor harimau.

CHAPTER 24

RELATIVE PRONOUNS

The relative pronouns are **yang, barangsiapa, apa, siapa** and **mana.**

Yang corresponds to the English relative pronouns 'who', 'which' and 'that'.

Barangsiapa and **apa** are independent relative pronouns, i.e. the nouns they refer back to are understood, not stated. (cf. 'Who steals my purse steals trash').

In English, a relative pronoun may be left out if it is the object of its clause. This can never happen in Indonesian.

Siapa (for persons) and **mana** (for animals and things) are used as relative pronouns after prepositions.

Orang *yang* telah menyapa kita adalah paman saya.
The man who spoke to us is my uncle.

Gadis *yang* kaulihat tadi adalah puteri walikota. The girl (whom) you saw just now is the mayor's daughter.

Itulah rumah *yang* kita cari. That is the house (that) we are looking for.

***Barangsiapa* mencuri adalah maling.** Who steals is a thief.

***Apa yang* telah saya dengar menghérankan saya.** What I have heard astonishes me.

Orang kepada *siapa* saya berikan uang itu adalah tukang-kebun saya. The man to whom I gave the money is my gardener.

Pacol dengan *mana* ia menggali lubang itu adalah punya saya. The spade with which he dug the hole is mine.

Note: The last two examples are very rarely used in every-day speech. We omit the relative pronouns and prepositions and use **yang** instead.

Orang *yang* saya beri uang itu adalah tukang-kebun saya.
The man that I gave the money (to) is my gardener.

Pacol *yang* dipakainya untuk menggali lubang itu adalah punya saya. The spade he used for digging the hole is mine.

The English possessive relative pronoun 'whose' is **yang** followed by the noun it qualifies, taking the suffix **-nya.**

Anak *yang* buku*nya* hilang itu adalah adik saya. The boy whose book was lost is my younger brother.

Anjing *yang* kaki*nya* patah itu adalah anjing tetangga kami. The dog the leg of which was broken is our neighbour's dog.

Rumah *yang* atap*nya* mérah itu akan dirombak. The house with the red roof (*lit.* the roof of which is red) will be broken up.

Note: As in English we also avoid the last clumsy example and we say instead:

Rumah yang beratap mérah itu akan dirombak. The house that has a red roof....

Likewise: **Anak *yang* baju*nya* baru itu....** The boy whose shirt is new....

becomes: **Anak *yang* berbaju baru itu....** The boy who wears a new shirt....

Again: **Orang *yang* kumis*nya* panjang itu....** The man whose moustache is long....

becomes: **Orang *yang* berkumis panjang itu....** The man who wears a long moustache....

The adverb of place **tempat** is used in the function of a relative pronoun in restrictive clauses. It is identical with the English relative adverb 'where'.

However, in Indonesian the antecedent (the noun it refers back to) of **tempat** may also be a person whom one asks, has confidence in, etc.

Kota *tempat* ia tinggal sangat sepi. The town where he lives is very quiet.

Rumah *tempat* kami mengadakan rapat akan dijual. The house where we held the meeting will be sold.

Orang *tempat* saya minta nasihat. The man of whom I asked advice.

Vocabulary

melahirkan to give birth to

mangkat to decease (of kings, noblemen, etc.)

wafat to decease (of holy people)

meninggal (dunia) to die (of ordinary people)

terlambat late (after appointed time)[1]

penggubah composer

terkenal well-known

pembuangan exile

pulau island

berkarang rocky

Lautan Atlantik Atlantic Ocean

rumah hantu haunted house

burung ketilang the Indonesian lark

sarang nest

Pangéran Diponegoro an Indonesian prince, leader of The Java War

pahlawan hero

gagah-berani courageous, brave

berbau to smell

busuk bad, awful

memperkenalkan to introduce

pésta feast

ulang-tahun birthday

singa lion

benua continent

bekas former, ex

mengunjungi to visit

téwas to perish, to be killed (in action, in battle)

pohon arén a kind of palm-tree

menakutkan horrifying

menceritakan to tell

ternyata to seem, appear

kabar bohong falsehood

pujangga poet

termasyhur famous

ditimpa to be struck, be deluged

banjir flood

terluka wounded

ditémbak mati to be shot, to be executed

tunangan fiancé

peperangan battle, war

penuh dengan full of

kutu busuk bug

mengalir to flow

dilayari to be navigated, navigable

terletak to be situated

di sebelah next to

timur east

di sebelah timur east of

Jawa Java

cendawan mushroom

beracun poisonous

memegang to hold, touch

---

[1] My *late* father, **Marhum (mendiang) ayahku.**

Exercise 24a

Add the relative pronoun to *the following:*

[1] Isteri Pak Saman, ... baru melahirkan anaknya yang ketujuh, meninggal dunia. [2] Ayahnya, ... telah pergi ke Tokyo, sudah kembali kemarin. [3] Keréta-api Jakarta-Surabaya, ... harus tiba jam 6.30, terlambat. [4] Saiful Bakhri, ... musiknya kaudengarkan tadi, adalah seorang penggubah Indonésia yang terkenal. [5] St. Heléna, ... pembuangan Napoléon Bonaparte adalah sebuah pulau berkarang yang kecil di Lautan Atlantik. [6].... berani tidur di rumah hantu itu akan mendapat hadiah Rp. 1000,—. [7] Burung ketilang, ... bersuara indah, membuat sarangnya di pohon arén. [8].... yang kami lihat sangat menakutkan. [9] Kabar.... kauceritakan kepada saya ternyata kabar bohong. [10] Désa.... pujangga termasyhur itu dilahirkan ditimpa banjir. [11] Kuda .... kakinya terluka itu telah ditémbak mati. [12] Gadis dengan.... ia menonton film adalah tunangannya.

Exercise 24b

Combine the following pairs of sentences by means of relative pronouns.

[1] *Pangéran Diponegoro* mangkat pada tahun 1855. *Beliau* adalah pahlawan yang gagah-berani.

[2] *Bunga* mati itu berbau busuk. Kautempatkan *bunga* itu di kamar saya seminggu yang lalu.

[3] Saya berjumpa dengan *temanmu*. Kamu memperkenalkan*nya* kepada saya di pésta ulang-tahun si Sien.

[4] *Singa* adalah binatang yang kuat. *Singa* hidup di benua Afrika.

[5] *Bekas guru saya* baru mengunjungi saya. *Putera guru* itu téwas dalam peperangan.

[6] *Kursi* ini penuh dengan kutu busuk. Saya duduk *di kursi* ini.

[7] *Sungai Musi* mengalir di Sumatera. *Sungai Musi* adalah sungai yang dapat dilayari kapal-kapal besar.

[8] *Pulau Bali* adalah pulau yang indah. *Pulau Bali* terletak di sebelah timur pulau Jawa.

[9] *Cendawan* itu beracun. Kaupegang *cendawan* itu tadi.

[10] *Orang* itu adalah kakak saya. Kamu baru bercakap-cakap dengan *orang* itu.

CHAPTER 25

SOME ARTICLES

We saw that Indonesian does not have articles corresponding to the English 'a' and 'the'. Instead we use **se** attached to a number—coefficient (which is actually the numeral one) and **itu** (which is actually a demonstrative pronoun). However, there are some words that are identical in meaning to 'a' and 'the', but they are only used in special cases. They are **yang, si, kaum** and **para** and are placed before the nouns they define.

Yang used with a positive adjective has the force of either a definite or indefinite article and turns the adjective into a noun, which denotes an individual person or thing or a group of persons (class) or things. English uses the propword 'one' (ones). Observe that **yang** is really a relative pronoun used here without antecedent.

Yang kuat **harus menolong** *yang lemah.*	The strong (who are strong) should help the weak (who are weak).
Berilah meréka *yang kecil.*	Give them the small one (ones).
Saya minta *yang baru.*	I want a new one.
Tidak ada *yang lain?*	Have you got no other ones?

Yang used with a comparative adjective is mostly indefinite.

Ia minta *yang lebih kecil.*	He wants *a* smaller one.
Ada *yang lebih baik?*	Have you got *a* better one?

Yang with a superlative adjective is usually definite.

Ia *yang tertua.*	He is *the* oldest.
Siapa *yang terakhir?*	Who was *the* last?
Inilah *yang paling besar.*	This is *the* biggest.

Yang is also used with ordinal numbers.

Siapa *yang pertama?*	Who was the first?
Amid *yang kedua.*	Amid is the second.

Tuan Harold beranak 5 orang. Yang *ketiga* dan yang *keempat* adalah anak kembar.	Mr. Harold has 5 children. The third and the fourth child are twins.

Note: The use of **yang** in the formation of demonstrative and interrogative pronouns.

yang itu	that one
yang ini	this one
yang mana?	which one?

Yang melamar pekerjaan itu tidak memenuhi syarat. Those who applied for the job did not fulfil the requirements.

Yang menyetujui usul Pak Wiro hendaknya mengacungkan tangannya. Those who second Pak Wiro's motion should put up their hands.

Yang diterima gembira, yang ditolak menyesal. Those who were accepted were happy, those who were rejected were disappointed.

Si as an article placed before an adjective converts the adjective into a noun. It does not denote a whole class or group of people but an individual typical of a class. To denote a whole class or a group of people **kaum** or **para** is used. **Kaum** may also be used with adjectives but **para** may be placed only before nouns.

si sakit	the sick man, the patient
si kaya	the rich man
si bodoh	the blockhead
kaum miskin	the poor
kaum cerdik pandai	the intellectuals, the intelligentsia
kaum ibu	the mothers

Si kaya bersenang-senang sedangkan kaum miskin membanting-tulang. The rich man enjoys himself while the poor wear themselves out.

para hadirin ladies and gentlemen (used in addressing an audience, *lit.* people who are present)

para orang-tua the parents

para martir the martyrs

Si may also be attached to nouns indicating the typical doer of an action. These nouns are mostly prefixed **pe** and are written as one word.

sipengirim	the sender	**sipenjahat**	the criminal
sipenerima	the recipient	**sipencuri**	the thief

CHAPTER 26

Dates and Letters
Hyphenation

The names of the months of the year are:

Januari	January	**Juli**	July
Pébruari	February	**Agustus**	August
Maret	March	**Séptémber**	September
April	April	**Oktober**	October
Mei	May	**Nopémber**	November
Juni	June	**Désémber**	December

The names of the days of the week are:

Minggu or **Ahad**	Sunday
Senin	Monday
Selasa	Tuesday
Rabu	Wednesday
Kamis	Thursday
Jumat	Friday
Sabtu	Saturday

Saturday evening or Saturday night is also called **malam Minggu** (cf. German Sonnabend).

In speech the word **bulan** often precedes the names of the months and **hari** precedes the names of the days.

Bulan apa sekarang?	What month is it now?
Sekarang bulan April.	It is now April.
Tanggal berapa sekarang?	What is the date now?
Sekarang tanggal 7 Juli.	It is now the 7th of July.
Kami akan mendapat libur dalam bulan Oktober.	We shall have holidays in October.
Ia akan berangkat ke Solo pada tanggal 11 bulan depan.	He will leave for Solo on the eleventh of next month.
Meréka akan pulang pada permulaan bulan Mei.	They will come home at the beginning of May.

Pada akhir bulan Januari.	At the end of January.
Pada pertengahan bulan Agustus.	Mid-August.
Hari apa sekarang?	What day is it to-day?
Sekarang hari Selasa.	It is now Tuesday.
Ia tiba pada hari Sabtu.	He arrived on Saturday.
tiap-tiap Minggu[1]	every Sunday.
Senin yang lalu.	last Monday.

Correspondence with people around the world is very interesting. Borders disappear and one gets to know about habits and customs of other people.

The Indonesian people consists of 200 ethnic groups, each one with characteristics of its own. The student is therefore strongly advised to have pen-friends in Indonesia and to exchange ideas with them. He might try to write a letter in Indonesian, and though he may make mistakes in the first two or three letters, linguistic mistakes are made to be corrected and not to be ashamed of. His Indonesian friends will certainly be willing to help improve his Indonesian. They are proud of their language and are always ready, if asked, to discuss points of usage.

How to write the letter

The address.

(a) In friendly letters no names of streets and numbers of houses are required. It is sufficient to write the name of the town and the date on the right hand top corner of the letter, e.g.

Dénpasar, 18 Ag. 198–

Note: The name of the town and the date are written on the same line; a comma is placed between them. Names of some months may be shortened. Jan. for Januari, Peb. for Pébruari, Ag. for Agustus, Sept. for Séptémber, Okt. for Oktober, Nop. for Nopémber and Des. for Désémber.

Figures may also be used instead of the names of the months, e.g. 18-8-198–, 7-2-198– or 18-8-'8–, 7-2-'8– (apostrophe is necessary when the figure of the year is shortened).

[1] however, **tiap-tiap minggu** (small 'm') is 'every week'.

(*b*) In business and formal letters the name of the recipient is placed under the date. The name and address of the firm sending the letter is written at the left-hand top corner and that of an individual who writes the letter under the complimentary close (see examples).

The Salutation
    (*a*) Friendly letters.

Kawanku yang baik,	My dear friend,
Kawanku Ali,	My friend Ali,
Sri yang baik,	Dear Sri,
Kawanku,	My friend,

    (*b*) Business and formal letters.

Dengan hormat,	Dear Sir, (*lit.* with respect)
Tuan yang terhormat,	Dear Sir,
Tuan Astono yang terhormat,	Dear Mr. Astono,

The Complimentary Close
    (*a*) Friendly

Salam dari,	Yours sincerely (*lit.* greetings from)
Salam hangat dari,	Yours very sincerely (*lit.* warm greetings from)
Sampaikan salamku kepada,	My regards to

    (*b*) Business and formal

Hormat kami.[1]	Yours truly (*lit.* our respect).
Hormat saya.	Yours truly (*lit.* my respect).
Wassalam.	Yours faithfully (*lit.* respect from)

Menunggu balasan Tuan, sebelumnya banyak terima kasih kami (saya) sampaikan. Awaiting your early reply, thanking you in anticipation.

---

[1] **hormat kami** is a complimentary note in a business letter, in which the signature is that of the director of the firm.
    hormat saya is a complimentary note in a private letter.

Harap Tuan maklum adanya. Hoping you will give this your attention.

Vocabulary

tg. abbreviation for **'tanggal'** (date)

kini now, at present

membalas to reply

sibuk busy

belajar to study

menghadapi ujian to sit for an examination

tata-buku bookkeeping

diadakan to be held

kesalahan mistake

lulus to pass

memperoléh to obtain

apakah if, whether

toko-buku bookstore

persediaan stock, supply

dékorasi rumah home-decoration

menaruh minat akan to be interested in

dengan with

sebagai as

bahan material

memberi kabar to inform (*lit.* give news)

harga price

mengenai about, concerning

berhubung dengan due to

ijazah certificate, diploma

memungkinkan to enable one to

masih still

bulu-tangkis badminton

berlatih to practise

perlu (adj.) necessary; (verb) to need

bagi to, for

mengingat with regard to

selingan change, intermezzo

méja-tulis writing table

angka figure, number

lagipula moreover

menyegarkan to refresh

badan body

nah! well!

sekian so far (used at the end of letters or speeches) →used instead of 'Thank you ladies and gentlemen' at the end of speeches; similarly used at the end of letters (cf. Latin 'dixi')

lagi again, more

bersama ini herewith

keterangan information

terlambatnya delay

pengiriman delivery

pesan order

terpaksa forcedly, unavoidably

mengabarkan kepada to inform

permintaan request, order

kabulkan, mengabulkan to grant

segera setelah as soon as

kali lain next time

memastikan to assure

mencukupi to fulfil
kertas-sampul wrapping-
paper
diproduksikan to be
produced

secara besar-besaran in
huge quantities
paberik-kertas paper-mill
langganan customer

Example of a friendly letter

Surabaya, 16 Maret 198–

Kawanky yang baik,

Banyak-banyak terima kasih akan suratmu tg. 21 Pébruari.
Maafkan bahwa aku baru kini dapat membalas suratmu itu. Aku
telah sibuk belajar untuk menghadapi ujian tata-buku yang telah
diadakan 5 hari yang lalu.

Untung aku dapat membuatnya dengan baik. Kukira aku
hanya membuat satu, dua kesalahan. Bila aku lulus aku akan
memperoléh ijazah tata-buku B, yang memungkinkan aku mencari pekerjaan di kantor yang lebih besar.

Kamu bertanya apakah aku masih tetap bermain bulu-tangkis.
Ya, aku berlatih dua kali seminggu, pada Selasa dan Sabtu soré.
Latihan ini perlu amat bagiku mengingat bahwa aku duduk
di méja-tulis berhari-harian menghadapi kertas-kertas, buku-buku
dan angka-angka. Maka bulu-tangkis merupakan selingan bagiku,
lagipula menyegarkan badanku.

Nah, sekian saja dahulu. Kali lain aku akan menulis lagi.
Sampaikan salamku kepada kedua orang-tuamu.

Salam dari kawanmu,
Husin.

Example of a formal letter

Médan, 14 Okt. 198–

Kepada
Toko Buku 'Aman'
Jl. Sulu 4,
BANDUNG.—

Dengan hormat,

Bersama ini saya minta keterangan apakah toko-buku
Tuan mempunyai persediaan buku-buku tentang dékorasi
rumah.

Saya menaruh minat akan dékorasi rumah dengan bambu sebagai bahan. Bila Tuan mempunyai buku-buku tersebut dapatlah Tuan memberi kabar kepada saya mengenai harganya.

Sebelumnya banyak terima kasih saya sampaikan.

Hormat saya,

H.L. Salim
Jl. Teuku Umar 27,
MEDAN.—

Example of a business letter.

P.T. 'KANCIL EMAS'   Jakarta, 2 Mei, 198–
   Pintu Air 57,
  JAKARTA.—
No.   : J/62/13.   Kepada
Hal   : Permintaan kertas sampul   P.T. Usaha Makmur
        No. 475.   Jl. Pecinan 15,
                                   SURABAYA.—

Tuan yang terhormat,

Berhubung dengan terlambatnya pengiriman kertas yang kami pesan dari Skandinavia maka terpaksa kami harus mengabarkan kepada Tuan bahwa permintaan Tuan dalam surat Tuan tg. 15 April 198– No. 47/83 tidak dapat kami kabulkan.

Segera setelah pengiriman dari Skandinavia itu tiba akan kami beri kabar kepada Tuan. Tetapi kami tidak dapat memastikan apakah kami dapat mencukupi permintaan Tuan, sebab kertas-sampul No. 475 yang Tuan minta itu tidak diproduksikan secara besar-besaran lagi oléh paberik kertas langganan kami di Skandinavia itu.

Harap Tuan maklum adanya.—

Hormat kami,
R.S. Mokhtar.
Direktur—

The Address:

```
Kepada Yth.
Tn. H. Waringan
Jl. Umpat 74,
KOTA BARU.—
```

Notes: **Yth.** is the abbreviation for **Yang terhormat** (*lit.* the most respected).

Tn. is the abbreviation for **Tuan.** Here are some other abbreviations:

Sdr., Saudara; Ny. Nyonya; Nn., Nona; Dr., Dokter; S.H., Sarjana Hukum (solicitor); **Ir., Insinyur** (engineer); **Jl., Jalan** (street), **Gg., Gang** (alley), **y.l., yang lalu** (last); **y.a.d., yang akan datang** (next); **dsb., dan sebagainya** (etc.).

In the address to a firm the abbreviation **Yth.** is usually left out

```
Kepada
Usaha Dagang 'ADIL'
Jl. Husin 17,
SOLO.—
```

Other forms of address and salutation:
—to the President of Indonesia:

Paduka Yang Mulia	Salutation:
Présiden Républik Indonésia	Paduka Yang Mulia,

—to ministers:

Yang Mulia Menteri....	Yang Mulia,
(the name of his ministry)	

—to governors:

Yang Mulia Gubernur...	Yang Mulia,
(the name of his province)	

—to mayors:

Yang terhormat Bapak Walikota....	
(the name of his town)	Bapak Walikota yang terhormat.

Hyphenation

When in print a word needs to be broken, hyphens are put between the syllables; after a prefix and before a suffix.

Examples:	**indah**	**in-dah**	splendid
	neraka	**ne-ra-ka**	hell
	menggambar	**meng-gam-bar**	to draw
	perkelahian	**per-ke-la-hi-an**	fight

h in the medial position, either silent or audible, is separated from the preceding letter.

Examples:	**dahan**	**da-han**	branch
	jahit	**ja-hit**	to sew
	sahut	**sa-hut**	answer
	pahit	**pa-hit**	bitter

ng followed by a vowel is separated from the preceding letter.

Examples:	**hangat**	**ha-ngat**	warm
	ingat	**i-ngat**	to remember
	singa	**si-nga**	lion

When it is followed by a consonant it remains attached to the preceding letter.

Examples:	**angka**	**ang-ka**	cipher
	tanggal	**tang-gal**	date
	sungguh	**sung-guh**	really

Diphthongs can be hyphenated only when they stand in closed syllables.

Examples:	**kain**	**ka-in**	cloth
	saing	**sa-ing**	to complete
	sauh	**sa-uh**	anchor
	daun	**da-un**	leaf
but:	**danau**	**da-nau**	lake
	ramai	**ra-mai**	noisy
	tirai	**ti-rai**	curtain

Exercise 26

Translate the following sentences into Indonesian:

[1] I have received your letter of July 15. [2] They will leave for London at the beginning of January. [3] Send my regards to your mother. [4] Are you interested in home-decoration? [5] Jack plays badminton every Saturday afternoon. [6] Could you inform me whether you have a supply of wrapping-paper? [7] Tono passed his examination last Tuesday. [8] When will the material be delivered? [9] That bookstore has a lot of customers. [10] I shall have holidays mid-June. [11] Why did not you reply my letter? [12] My father will come home in March.

CHAPTER 27

PREPOSITIONS

Two important prepositions are **di** (in, at, on) and **ke** (to). Other prepositions are derived from them:

di kamar	in the room
di sekolah	at school
di méja	on the table
ke kantor	to the office
ke geréja	to church
di Berlin	in Berlin
ke Hong Kong	to Hong Kong

Attached to nouns denoting place such as **belakang** (back), **muka** (front), **samping** (side) **di** and **ke** make new prepositions. The combination **di**+*noun* expresses movement in a place of rest, while **ke**+*noun* expresses movement from place to place.

Examples:

Ia berjalan di dalam taman.	She walked in (within) the park.
Murid-murid masuk ke dalam ruang kelas.	The pupils came into the classroom.
Anjing itu berbaring di bawah méja.	The dog is lying under the table.
Marilah kita lari ke bawah pohon itu.	Let us run to (under) that tree.
Si Urip di belakang rumah.	Urip is behind the house.
Saya pergi ke belakang garasi.	I went to the back of the garage.
Kucing itu memanjat ke atas atap.	The cat climbed on (to) the roof.
Kera itu duduk di atas atap.	The monkey sat on the roof.

These prepositions become adverbs when they are not associated with any other words, e.g.

Meréka naik ke atas.	They went up.
Saya tinggal di sebelah.	I live next door.
Anak-anak bermain-main di luar.	The children are playing outside.

The following are prepositions formed from **di** and **ke:**

di samping	beside
ke samping	aside
di dekat	near
ke dekat	over by
di muka, di depan	in front of
ke muka, ke depan	to the front of
di seberang	opposite, across
ke seberang	across
di sekitar	in the vicinity of
ke sekitar	to the vicinity of
di tengah	in the centre of
ke tengah	to the centre of

In English a verb-root or an adjective may sometimes be replaced by one transitive verb, e.g. to look for = to seek. In Indonesian there are a few verb-roots or adjectives that can become simply transitive by the addition of affixes to the root-verbs and by the omission of the prepositions.

cinta pada →mencintai	to love
Ia cinta padanya. ⎫ **Ia mencintainya.** ⎭	He loved her.
benci pada →membenci	to hate
Meréka benci pada orang itu. ⎫ **Meréka membenci orang itu.** ⎭	They hated that man.
marah pada →memarahi	to be angry with
Ia marah padaku. ⎫ **Ia memarahi aku.** ⎭	He was angry with me.
suka akan →menyukai	to like (things)
suka pada →menyukai	to like (people)

Anak itu suka akan mangga mentah. **Anak itu menyukai mangga mentah.**	That boy likes unripe mangoes.
Saya suka padanya. **Saya menyukainya.**	I like him.

percaya pada →mempercayai — to believe, to trust
Meréka tak percaya padaku. — They do not believe me.
Saya tak mempercayainya. — I do not trust him.

insaf akan, sadar akan →menginsafi menyadari — to realize
Ia insaf akan kesalahannya. — He realized his mistakes
Kamu seharusnya menyadari bahaya perjalanan itu. — You should realize the dangers of the journey.

kawin dengan →mengawini — to marry

Ia kawin dengan seorang janda. **Ia mengawini seorang janda.**	He married a widow.

tahu akan →mengetahui — to know (things)
kenal pada →mengenal — to know (people)
ingat akan (pada) →mengingat — to remember
lupa akan →melupakan — to forget
rindu akan →merindukan — to long for
tertawa akan →menertawakan — to laugh at
harap akan →mengharapkan — to hope for
ingin akan →menginginkan — to wish for

Some prefixed words can also be freed from their prepositions.

berjumpa dengan →menjumpai — to meet with
bertemu dengan →menemui — to meet with
bertanya pada →menanyai — to ask to[1]

memberi hormat pada **memberi salam pada**	→**menghormati**	to greet, to pay respect to

Ask him if he wants coffee.	*Tanya* **padanya apakah ia mau kopi.**
Ask him for a cup of coffee.	*Minta* **padanya secangkir kopi.**

Exercise 27

Insert the right preposition in the blank spaces below.

dari, from, of; **dengan,** with; **tanpa,** without; **sejak,** since; **selama,** during; **pada,** at, on; **(ke)pada,** to; **bagi, untuk,** for; **hingga, sampai,** till; **tentang,** about; **sepanjang,** along; **di antara,** among, between; **melalui,** past, through; **oléh,** by; **karena,** because of; **kecuali,** except; **menjelang,** towards (time); **menuju ke,** towards (place, abstract nouns); **di,** in, at, on; **ke,** to.

[1] Saya pergi.... sekolah tiap-tiap hari. [2] Kakaknya tinggal ....rumah. [3] Kami tidak mengetahui apa-apa.... hal itu. [4] Pak Hasan bekerja.... kantornya.... jam empat soré. [5] Meréka berkendaraan.... pantai. [6] Anak itu meninggalkan kelas.... minta ijin.... gurunya. [7] Bunga ini.... saya? [8].... dinding itu tergantung sebuah loncéng kuno. [9] Berjuta-juta orang téwas ....Perang Dunia II. [10] Semboyan meréka adalah 'Mengembara.... kebahagiaan'. [11] Pasukan kami berjalan.... pagi tadi. [12].... soré hari hujan berhenti. [13] Dongéng itu dikarang.... seorang pengarang yang masyhur. [14] Terjadilah perselisihan ....anggota-anggota regu itu. [15] Semua hadir.... pertemuan itu.... Tuan Harijaya. [16] Pak Sumo tidak dapat berjalan cepat.... usianya yang lanjut. [17] Angin kencang menghembus ....Selatan. [18] Pemburu itu memasuki hutan.... lima ékor anjing-pemburu. [19] Ada pesanan.... Tuan Diréktur. [20] Jangan berjalan.... lorong itu sesudah gelap.

CHAPTER 28

CONJUNCTIONS

A conjunction is a word such as 'and', 'or', 'but' which joins words, clauses or sentences. The Indonesian conjunction has the same function as the English conjunction.

Examples:

Mini menyanyi *dan* Irma bermain piano. Mini sang *and* Irma played the piano.
Yang hitam *atau* yang putih? The black one *or* the white one?
Itu tidak sukar, *tetapi* mudah. It is not difficult, *but* easy.

The following is a fairly complete list of conjunctions:

ketika, waktu	when (at the moment that, during the time that)
kalau, jika	when (whenever, on any occasion that)
bila, andaikata	if
karena, oléh karena, sebab	as, for, because
sebelum	before
setelah, sesudah	after
segera setelah	as soon as
sejak	since
hingga, sampai	till, until
sedang, selama	while
agar, supaya, agar supaya	so that, in order that
meskipun, walaupun	though, although
asal, asalkan, asal saja	provided
seperti, seakan-akan, seolah-olah	as if
bahwa	that

Examples:

Ketika ia menyeberang jalan, ia ditubruk oléh mobil.
When he was crossing the street he was run over by a car.

Saya masih kanak-kanak *waktu* perang pecah. I was only a child *when* the war broke out.

Kami tidak akan datang, *bila* hujan. We will not come *if* it rains.

Andaikata ia tahu, ia tidak akan bertanya. *If* he knew he would not have asked.

Anton tidak pergi ke sekolah, *karena* ia sakit. Anton did not go to school *because* he was ill.

Sebab kami lelah, kami beristirahat. *As* we were tired we took a rest.

Meréka bekerja *hingga* meréka lelah. They worked *till* they were tired.

Vocabulary

berusaha	to endeavour, do one's utmost
melarang	to forbid
on notices,	
dilarang merokok	no smoking allowed
dilarang masuk	no entry
dilarang membuang kotoran di sini	deposit no refuse here
perkakas	tool, instrument
memerintah	to order, govern
bertindak	to act, take measures
obat	medicine
mengira	to suppose
memakai	to use

Exercise 28

Fill up:

[1] Meskipun anak itu berusaha, ...

[2] Meskipun hujan, ...

[3] Walaupun si Kadir dilarang pergi, ...

[4] Walaupun ia kaya, ...
[5] Meréka berkata itu, seolah-olah . . . .
[6] Ia memakai perkakas saya, seolah-olah . . . .
[7] Kami diperintahnya, seakan-akan . . . .
[8] Perempuan itu bertindak, seakan-akan . . . .
[9] Kamu boléh bermain-main di sini, asalkan . . . .
[10] Pak Hasan minum obat, agar supaya . . . .
[11] Ia sedih, sebab . . . .   . .
[12] Si Murti mengira bahwa . . . .

CHAPTER 29

INTERJECTIONS

Like its English equivalent the Indonesian interjection may be a word or a phrase that has no grammatical relation to a sentence.

Wah! is used to express surprise, astonishment or fear.

> **Wah! Bagus!**   Oh! That's fine!
> **Wah! Kalungku hilang!**   O! My necklace is gone!

Hai! is used to call attention or to express joy, wonder, or interrogation.

> **Hai! Kamu menunggu siapa?**   Hey! Whom are you waiting for?
> **Hai! Kapan kamu datang?**   Hey! When did you arrive?

Aduh! is used to express pain or pity.

> **Aduh! Sakitnya!**   Oh! How painful!
> **Aduh! Lihat, anak kecil itu buta.**   Oh! Look, that little child is blind.

Masya Allah! is used to express surprise or wonder.

> **Orang itu telah kawin untuk keenam kalinya.**   That man has married for the sixth time.
> **Masya Allah!**   Good heavens!

Ayuh! Mari! are used to express invitation.

> **Ayuh, kita pergi sekarang.**   Shall we go now? (Come, let us go now.)
> **Mari!**   Come on!
> **Mari makan!**   Let's have dinner!

Masa! Masakan! are used to express doubt.

> **Pak Amir menang loteré.**   Pak Amir has won a lottery.
> **Masa?**   Really?

Ia belajar bahasa Inggeris dari kamus. He learns English from dictionaries.

Masakan? Really?

Celaka! is used to express irritation or dissatisfaction.

> **Celaka! Ban sepédaku kempis!** Damn! The tyre of my bike is flat.

Oh! is used to express disappointment.

> **Oh! Keréta-api akan datang terlambat!** Oh! The train will come late.

Sayang! Kasihan! are used to express regret and pity respectively.

> **Kami datang terlambat, sayang!** We came too late, I'm afraid.
>
> **Kasihan! Anak itu baru kehilangan orang-tuanya.** How sad! That child has just lost its parents.

Astaga! is used to express amazement.

> **Astaga! Kamu bangun jam sembilan tadi pagi?** Dear me! You woke at nine this morning?

Ah! Akh! are used to express dislike, disagreement or anger.

> **Ah! Orang semacam dia!** Bah! Such a fellow.
>
> **Akh! Jangan mengganggu saya.** Ah! Don't disturb me. Leave me alone!

Vocabulary

air	water	**bola-dunia**	globe
tenggelam	to drown	**kutub**	pole
tuli	deaf	**juga**	also
memancing	to fish	**begitu**	so, quite
pil-tidur	sleeping-pill	**pelancong**	traveller
demikian	so, that	**berbaring**	to lie
memutar-mutar	to turn round and round	**ambang-pintu**	threshold
pényék	flattened	**malas**	lazy
		lebih suka	to prefer

saja 1 only. **Harganya serupiah saja.** It costs only a
rupiah.

2 nothing but. **Ia makan sayuran saja.** He eats only
vegetables.

3 continuously. **Gadis itu kemarin menangis saja.**
The girl was crying continuously yesterday.

4 even. **Duduk saja ia tak dapat, apalagi berdiri.**
She can't even sit up, let alone stand up.

5 any, ever (used to modify a request, etc.) **Siapa saja
boléh datang.** Any one may come.
Ke mana saja saya pergi, ia mengikuti saya.
Wherever I go he follows me.

Exercise 29

Translate the following anecdotes (lelucon) *into English:*

Polisi: 'Hai, dilarang berenang di sungai ini!'
Orang yang berada di dalam air: 'Saya tak berenang, saya
tenggelam.'

Dua orang tuli berjumpa di jalan.
Amat: 'Hai Min, kamu pergi memancing?'
Amin: 'Tidak, aku pergi memancing.'
Amat: 'Oh, kukira kamu akan pergi memancing.'

'Inilah pil-tidur Nyonya. Cukup untuk tiga minggu.'
'Astaga! Saya tidak mau tidur demikian lama.'

Pak Guru memutar-mutar bola-dunia yang terletak di méjanya,
dan kemudian bertanya pada murid-muridnya mengapa bumi
agak pényék pada kedua kutub.
Si Parto yang mengira bahwa Pak Guru memandangnya, berkata: 'Sungguh-sungguh bukan saya yang membuatnya Pak,
kemarin juga sudah begitu!'

Seorang pelancong melihat anjingnya berbaring di ambang-
pintu.
'Ayuh, anjing malas,' katanya, 'kita berangkat sekarang.'
'Ah, saja lebih suka tidur saja,' jawab anjing itu.

CHAPTER 30

REPORTED SPEECH

1 *Statement*
2 *Question*
3 *Imperative*

As Indonesian has no tenses corresponding with those of European languages reported speech is not as complicated as in English. The verb in direct speech undergoes no changes when put in reported speech. The only thing that should be noticed is the change of person. The clause is always introduced by the conjunction **bahwa** (that), which can never be left out in reported statements.

> **Ia berkata, 'Saya sakit.'**   She said, 'I am ill.'
> **Ia berkata bahwa ia sakit.**   She said (that) she was ill.
> **Meréka menjawab, 'Kami belum menonton film itu.'** They answered, 'We haven't seen that film yet.'
> **Meréka menjawab bahwa meréka belum menonton film itu.** They answered (that) they had not seen that film yet.

When the reported verb in direct speech is placed at the end of the sentence it is always regarded as a noun, therefore the prefix **me-** or **ber-** is left out and the subject becomes a possessive. Often, the reported verb in reported speech is put in the passive, especially with **nya** as agent.

> **'Orang itu berdusta,' katanya.**   'That man lied,' said he (was *his statement*).
> **Dikatakannya bahwa orang itu berdusta.** He said (that) that man had lied. (*It was said* by him.)
> **'Saya tak tahu,' jawab Ali.**   'I don't know,' answered Ali. (was *Ali's answer*).
> **Dijawabnya bahwa ia tak tahu.** He answered that he did not know. (*It was answered* by him.)

Thus we find a few cases of reported speech that begin with:

diduganya bahwa....	he presumed that (it was presumed by him that)....
dikiranya bahwa....	he supposed that....
disangkanya bahwa....	he surmised that....
dipikirnya bahwa....	he thought that....
dianggapnya bahwa....	he regarded that....

However, with the other persons and with nouns we prefer to use the active form.

Saya menduga bahwa   **Kamu mengira bahwa....**
   (I presumed that)....   **Kita memikir bahwa....**
Akhmad menyangka
   bahwa....
Meréka menganggap
   bahwa....

bahwa is mostly left out when the introducing word of the clause is a question word.

Orang itu bertanya padaku, 'Di mana rumahmu?'
That man asked me, 'Where do you live?'
Orang itu bertanya di mana rumahku.   That man asked where I lived.
'Kapan kamu berangkat?' tanya meréka.   'When are you leaving?' they asked.
Meréka ingin tahu kapan kami berangkat.   They wanted to know when we were leaving.

The clause of a reported question which has no question word is introduced by **apakah** (cf. English 'whether', 'if').

Pak Guru bertanya, 'Kamu sudah mempelajari bab dua?'
Pak Guru bertanya apakah kami sudah mempelajari bab dua.
The teacher asked, 'Have you studied chapter two yet?'
The teacher asked if we had studied chapter two.

'Kamu suka nasi goréng?' tanyanya.
Ia bertanya apakah saya suka nasi goréng.
'Do you like fried rice?' he asked.
He asked if I like fried rice.

Imperatives are reported by the verbs: **menyuruh,** to order; **memerintahkan,** to command.

Pergilah!	Go!
Ia menyuruh saya pergi.	He ordered me to go.

Requests are reported by the verbs: **mempersilakan,** to request; **minta,** to ask.

Masuklah!	Come in!
Ia mempersilakan kami masuk.	He asked us to come in.

Negative imperatives are reported by the verb: **melarang,** to forbid.

Jangan minum air itu.	Don't drink that water.
Ia melarang saya minum air itu.	He forbade me to drink that water.

In English we may negative the infinitive, e.g. 'He asked me not to go'. Indonesian usually puts the negative on the introducing verb: **'Ia *tidak memperboléhkan* saya pergi.'** ('He does not allow me to go.')

Vocabulary

lampu-sepéda bicycle-lamp	**seru** to call out
mencuri to steal	**ujar** to speak
keséhatan health	**selesai** to finish, finished
menunggu to wait	**menyelesaikan** to finish (trans.)
lama long (of duration)	
panjang long (of measurement)	**melakukan** to do
pegang to hold	**ada pertanyaan?** any questions?

Exercise 30

Put the following sentences into Reported Speech.

[1] Ia berkata, 'Lampu-sepéda saya dicuri orang.'
[2] Saya bertanya kepada Kusin, 'Bagaimana dengan keséhatanmu?'
[3] 'Kami tidak mau menunggu terlalu lama,' kata si Jayus.
[4] 'Apa yang kaupegang itu?' tanya Pak Marto kepadaku.
[5] Ia berkata kepadaku, 'Saya tidak kenal padanya.'
[6] 'Pergilah!' serunya kepada pengemis itu.
[7] 'Duduklah!' ujarnya pada kami.
[8] Kamu mengatakan, 'Kami telah selesai dengan pekerjaan kami.'
[9] 'Siapa gadis itu?' tanya si Polan.
[10] Ia memerintahkan kepadaku, 'Jangan ke luar!'
[11] Saya menjawab, 'Bukan saya yang melakukan itu.'
[12] Pak Guru bertanya, 'Ada pertanyaan?'

CHAPTER 31

THE WORDS *ADA* AND *ADALAH*

The word **ada** has a variety of meanings. It is used to introduce a sentence the subject of which is indefinite. The English equivalent is 'there is', 'there are', 'there will be', etc.

Ada pondok di kaki bukit itu.	There is a hut at the foot of the hill.
Ada tamu.	There is a visitor.
Akan ada pertandingan sépakbola minggu depan.	There will be a football match next week.
Tidak ada apa-apa.	There is nothing doing. There is nothing in particular. There is nothing wrong.
Ada sesuatu yang akan kutanyakan kepadamu.	There is something I want to ask you about.

Ada also means 'to possess', 'to have in stock'.

Saya ada persediaan semén.	I have a supply of cement.
Ada berapa sak?	How many sacks have you?
Ada sabun 'Bintang'?	Have you 'Bintang' soap?
Tidak ada.	We have not.
Ada padamu lima rupiah?	Have you five rupiahs with you?

The English 'be in a place' is **ada** in Indonesian. It is sometimes prefixed **ber-**.

Ia ada di rumah.	He is at home.
Tuan Bliss ada?	Is Mr. Bliss in?
Ada.	Yes, he is in.
Ia ada di mana sekarang?	Where is he now?
Ia berada di Jakarta.	He is in Jakarta.

When we want to emphasize a verb we place **ada** before it. English uses the emphatic 'do'.

> **Saya ada menerima surat.** I did receive a letter.
> **Ia ada mengatakan itu**   He did tell me so.
> **kepadaku.**
> **Meréka ada mempunyai**   They do have a motor car.
> **mobil.**

Some useful phrases, derivatives and expressions with **ada.**

> **ada-ada saja** something new again.
> **adanya** 1 used at the beginning of a sentence introduces a fact or circumstance that is known to exist.
> **Adanya barang-barang berharga di rumah Pak Kasim menimbulkan dugaan bahwa ia telah mencurinya.** The fact that there are many valuable items at Pak Kasim's house arouse suspicion of his having stolen them.
> 2 used at the end of a sentence, especially a good wish, which means 'may it be so'.
> **Semoga kamu séhat adanya.** I wish you good health (let it be so).
> **Demikianlah adanya.** Such is the fact, so are the facts; used to finish a letter or story.

Adapun As to, concerning
Adapun surat Tuan.... With reference to your letter....
Ada apa? What's the matter?
Makanlah seada-adanya. Would you care to take 'pot luck' with us? (*lit*. Eat what is served.)
mengadakan to arrange, bring about, establish.
Kami mengadakan pésta. We arranged a party (feast).
Meréka mengadakan damai. They made peace.
Negarawan-negarawan itu mengadakan mupakat. The statesmen reached agreement.
keadaan situation, fact, condition, state.
Gadis itu dalam keadaan pingsan. The girl was in a state of unconsciousness.

Ada gula, ada semut (proverb). As long as one can afford to keep open house, one will have visitors. (*lit.* Where there is sugar, there are ants.)

adalah

'to be'+noun is **adalah**+*noun*. It is used mostly in long sentences. Synonymous to **adalah** is **ialah.**

Examples:

Meréka adalah peziarah yang datang dari segenap penjuru dunia. They are pilgrims who come from all parts of the world.

Yang diharapkan oléh pedagang-pedagang itu adalah keuntungan. What the traders had hoped for was profit.

Makanan utama penduduk pulau kecil itu ialah jagung. The staple diet of the inhabitants of that small island is corn.

Orang itu ialah bekas opsir angkatan udara. That man is an ex-officer of the air force.

adalah also opens sentences in stories and fables. It corresponds to the English 'there was once'.

Examples:

Adalah seorang puteri raja yang sangat cantik. There was once a beautiful princess.

Adalah seorang raja yang amat kejam. There was once a very cruel king.

Adalah sebuah kerajaan yang makmur. There was once a prosperous kingdom.

Conversation

DI TOKO — AT THE SHOP

A.: **Ada rokok 'Durian'?** A.: Have you 'Durian' cigarettes?

B.: **Ada. Pakai berapa pak?** B.: Yes, we have. How many packages?

A.: **Tiga pak.** A.: Three, please.

B.: **Apa lagi?** B.: Anything else?

A.: **Ada korék?**

A.: Have you got matches?

B.: **Maaf. Kami kekurangan korék déwasa ini. Seminggu lagi mungkin kami mendapat persediaan baru.**

B.: Sorry. We are short of matches at the moment. In a week's time we get a new supply.

A.: **Saya mencari sabun-mandi 'Inda'. Dimana-mana tak ada. Tuan ada beberapa?**

A.: I am looking for 'Inda' soap. It is nowhere to be had. Have you got any?

B.: **Oh, sabun itu sudah lama tidak ada di toko-toko. Tuan mau 'Dalia' sebagai gantinya?**

B.: Oh, that soap hasn't been at the shops for a long time. Do you want 'Dalia' instead?

A.: **Berapa harganya?**

A.: What's the price?

B.: **Seratus rupiah.**

B.: One hundred rupiah.

A.: **Begitu mahal?**

A.: As expensive as that?

B.: **Ya, mémang harga-harga barang banyak naik belakangan ini. Tuan mau pakai?**

B.: Yes, prices of goods have gone up much lately. Do you want any?

A.: **Berilah saya dua buah. Jadi berapa semuanya?**

A.: Give me two, please. How much is it altogether?

B.: **Dua ratus tujuhpuluh lima rupiah.**

B.: Two hundred and seventy-five rupiahs.

CHAPTER 32

IT

'It', the much-used English impersonal pronoun has no Indonesian equivalent. Let us discuss the various uses of 'it' in English and consider their translation into Indonesian. In sentences with 'it is' used for emphasis, where English uses 'who' after the subject, Indonesian attaches the emphatic **lah** to the subject and the word **yang** follows.

Sayalah yang telah melihatnya.	It is I who have seen it.
Didilah yang menjerit tadi.	It was Didi who has just shouted.
Dialah yang setuju.	It is he who has agreed.

It as a provisional subject

(*a*) When the real subject is contained in a following clause which has another subject, *it* is omitted. The form is: adjective + **bagi**

> *Perlu bagi* **kita mengetahuinya.** It is *necessary that* we should know it.
>
> *Penting bagi***mu menjawab surat itu.** It is important that you answer that letter.

Observe that **bagi** = for

The English sentences may be rendered by the form:
>   It is necessary for us to....
>   It is important for you to....

The following example cannot be so changed.

It is clear that she does not want to go with us.

In this case we use **bahwa** after the adjective, and a subject follows. Often the emphatic **lah** is attached to the adjective.

Jelaslah bahwa ia tak mau ikut dengan kita.

Likwise: **Teranglah bahwa ia bersalah.** It is obvious that he was guilty.

When the main clause is in the passive form: *it is said, it is believed*, Indonesian also uses the passive: **dikatakan, diduga** + **bahwa.**

Dikatakan bahwa ia telah terbunuh. It was said that he was murdered.

Diduga bahwa kita akan mendapat hujan. It is believed that we shall have rain.

(*b*) When the real subject is an infinitive, Indonesian uses the form: adjective+verb.

Séhat bangun pagi-pagi. It is healthy to wake up early.

Gampang mengatakan itu. It is easy to say that.

Sometimes the preposition **untuk** precedes the verb.

Sukar untuk memecahkan soal itu. It is difficult to solve the problem.

Similarly, when the real subject is a verbal noun.

Tidak ada gunanya (untuk) menunggu di sini. It is no use waiting here.

It used with an impersonal verb is left out in Indonesian.

Hujan It is raining.

Hujan rintik-rintik, gerimis. It is drizzling.

Remarks on the weather are often introduced with **hari** (day), **hawa** (weather, air), **cuaca** (weather).

Dingin or **Hari dingin.**   It is cold.
Panas or **Hawa panas.**   It is warm.
Gelap or **Cuaca gelap.**   It is dark.

Vocabulary

bersatu teguh, bercerai runtuh united we stand, divided we fall

melalaikan to neglect

memperoléh to gain

keuntungan profit

perselisihan quarrel, dispute

bagian part, department, section

warisan inheritance

kematian death

memperingatkan to warn

terhadap against

semacam such

berkumpul to gather	**satu demi satu, satu per**
tongkat stick	**satu** one by one
terikat tied	**susah payah** trouble, labour
erat tight(ly)	**tak usah** no need to
ujar to say	**takut akan** to be afraid of
toh yet, still	**kedurjanaan** evil, malice
kekuatan strength	**musuh** enemy
mematahkan to break	**lantai** floor
sekuat tenaga with might	**membandingkan** to
and main	compare

Exercise 32

BERSATU TEGUH

Seorang petani berputera tujuh orang. Putera-putera itu sering berkelahi dan karena perkelahian-perkelahian itu meréka melalaikan pekerjaan meréka. Di dusun itu ada beberapa orang jahat; meréka hendak memperoléh keuntungan dari perselisihan anak-anak laki-laki itu dan mengharapkan bagian warisan setelah kematian ayah meréka.

Ayah itu insaf akan hal ini dan hendak memperingatkan putera-puteranya terhadap orang-orang semacam itu.

Pada suatu hari iapun menyuruh semua puteranya datang berkumpul. Sekarang ia meletakkan di muka pemuda-pemuda itu tujuh batang tongkat yang terikat erat menjadi satu.

'Anak-anak', demikian ujarnya kepada meréka, 'kaulihat ikatan tongkat ini? Cobalah kekuatanmu; bila kamu berhasil mematahkannya akan kubayar seratus rupiah'.

Masing-masing mencobanya. Putera-putera itu berusaha sekuat tenaga, tetapi tak seorangpun berhasil. Akhirnya berkatalah meréka: 'Sekali-kali tak mungkin.'

Kata ayah itu: 'Toh tak ada barang yang lebih gampang.' Ia melepaskan tongkat-tongkat itu dari ikatannya dan mematahkannya sebatang demi sebatang tanpa susah payah.

'Kalau begitu mudah saja!' seru putera-puteranya, 'kalau demikian saja seorang anakpun dapat melakukannya.'

Ujar ayah itu: 'Nah, apa yang terjadi dengan tongkat-tongkat ini akan terjadi pula dengan dirimu. Bila kamu bersatu teguh, maka kamu tak usah takut akan kedurjanaan musuh-musuhmu.

Tetapi bila kamu bercerai, maka dengan mudah juga akan terjadi dengan dirimu seperti tongkat-tongkat yang patah terletak di lantai ini.'

Answer the following questions in Indonesian :

[1] Berapakah putera petani itu?

[2] Apa sebabnya meréka melalaikan pekerjaan meréka?

[3] Apakah yang diharapkan orang-orang jahat di dusun itu?

[4] Ayah itu akan memperingatkan putera-puteranya terhadap apa?

[5] Apakah yang diletakkan oléh ayah itu di depan putera-puteranya? Dan apa pula yang diperintahkannya kepada meréka?

[6] Siapakah dari meréka yang berhasil mematahkan ikatan tongkat-tongkat itu?

[7] Bagaimanakah cara petani itu mematahkan tongkat-tongkat itu?

[8] Pemuda-pemuda itu berseru bagaimana?

[9] Petani itu membandingkan ikatan tongkat-tongkat itu dengan apa?

[10] Apakah yang akan terjadi bila putera-putera itu bercerai?

KEY TO THE EXERCISES

Exercise 2a

Possible sentences are:

Mesin ini rusak. Pemburu itu menémbak harimau. Ini bénsin, bukan minyak-tanah. Siapa kamu? Nyonya Jones datang dari London. Keréta-api itu berangkat jam empat. Tak seorang menjawab. Ibu menggoréng ikan. Itu Jalan Mawar. Serdadu menangkap pencuri itu. Emas logam. Hari ini Rabu. Tiap anak mendapat coklat. Air ini kotor. Ali dan Akhmad bersaudara.

Exercise 2b

[1] He stole a clock. [2] That goat is eating grass. [3] This table is light. [4] This knife is not sharp. [5] Akhmad killed a snake. [6] The hunter bathed in the river. [7] This clock is too fast. [8] The servant cut grass with a knife. [9] This garden is very fine. [10] Ali is eating a banana. [11] Who made this table? [12] That is a hedge. [13] The hedge is not fine. [14] This snake is poisonous. [15] He sold a goat. [16] The servant is very old.

Exercise 3a

[1] Kursi ini. [2] Dokter pandai itu. [3] Rumah kami yang kecil. [4] Itu unta. [5] Adik saya nakal. [6] Ini dinding bambu. [7] Kapal-terbang kami mendarat. [8] Listrik mati. [9] Dokter memeriksa saya. [10] Itu menarik. [11] Kacamata saya patah. [12] Kakak saya terlambat. [13] Ini kursi jurutik. [14] Isteri sopir meréka sakit. [15] Orang itu pelaut. [16] Jurutik baru itu bodoh.

Exercise 3b

[1] Ini kakak saya. [2] Murid rajin itu naik kelas. [3] Negara meréka sangat kaya. [4] Polisi itu menangkap pencuri. [5] Hidung orang itu berdarah. [6] Paman Peter dokter-gigi. [7] Film itu menarik. [8] Anak Tuan Smith sakit. [9] Ini rumah saya. [10] Orang yang kuat dan séhat itu gembira.

Exercise 4

[1] Ibu tidak (tiada, tak) menjemur pakaian. [2] Ali tidak pergi ke sekolah. [3] Ayah tidak membelikan saya sepasang sepatu. [4] Ini bukan kemenakan saya. [5] Kamus ini tidak mahal. [6] Orang itu bukan Pak Hasan. [7] Kami belum melihat film itu. [8] Saya tidak suka tomat. [9] Bukan Nora yang merobék gambar itu. [10] Tetangga kami belum kembali dari Éropa. [11] Suami saya tidak di rumah. [12] Ini bukan berlian. [13] Ia belum menjual mesin-jahit itu. [14] Bukan saya yang menyapa kamu di kantorpos.

Exercise 5

[1] Kamu kenal padanya? Apakah kamu kenal padanya? Kenalkah kamu padanya? [2] Kamu haus? Apakah kamu haus? Hauskah kamu? [3] Meréka gembira? Apakah meréka gembira? Gembirakah meréka? [4] Ini bukan tas ayahmu? Apakah ini bukan tas ayahmu? Bukankah ini tas ayahmu? [5] Anak ini pandai? Apakah anak ini pandai? Pandaikah anak ini? [6] Ibunya sudah sembuh? Apakah ibunya sudah sembuh? Sudahkah ibunya sembuh? or Sudah sembuhkah ibunya? [7] Kamu mau pergi dengan saya? Apakah kamu mau pergi dengan saya? Mau-kah kamu pergi dengan saya? [8] Tuan dokter? Apakah Tuan dokter? Dokterkah Tuan? [9] Pak Amat tukang-kebun? Apakah Pak Amat tukang-kebun? Tukang-kebunkah Pak Amat? [10] Kamu sudah makan? Apakah kamu sudah makan? Sudahakah kamu makan?

Exercise 7a

[1] Itu jakét siapa? Jakét siapakah itu? [2] Ia tinggal di mana? Di manakah ia tinggal? [3] Perempuan itu menangis mengapa? Apa sebabnya perempuan itu menangis? [4] Tinggi menara itu berapa? Berapakah tinggi menara itu? [5] Kamu makan apa? Apa yang kamu makan? [6] Namanya siapa? Siapakah namanya? [7] Mantel ini punya siapa? Punya siapakah mantel ini? [8] Meréka pindah kapan? Bilamana meréka pindah? [9] Lusa hari libur? Apakah lusa hari libur? [10] Ini buku apa? Buku apakah ini? [11] Ini punyamu? Apakah ini punyamu? [12] Orang itu siapa? Siapakah orang itu? [13] Harga lampu ini berapa? Berapa-kah harga lampu ini? [14] Uangmu mana? Mana uangmu? [15]

Ayahmu pergi ke Tokyo kapan? Kapankah ayahmu pergi ke Tokyo? [16] Kamu tiba jam berapa? Jam berapakah kamu tiba?

Exercise 7b

[1] Ya, saya dapat menyanyi. Tidak, saya tidak dapat menyanyi. [2] Ibukota Perancis adalah Paris. [3] Ya, saya dapat berbahasa Indonésia. [4] Karena saya sakit. [5] Umur saya duapuluh lima tahun. [6] Karena merokok dapat menyebabkan kangker. [7] Kamu dapat membeli perangko di kantorpos. [8] Tukang-potong-rambut. [9] Saya menulis dengan pulpén. [10] Pertunjukan mulai jam delapan. [11] Ia lari ke gang. [12] Saya membaca berita tentang pembunuhan. [13] Ia minta és. [14] Ini payung Muna. [15] Saya membeli cincin berlian itu. [16] Ia memukul saya tiga kali.

Exercise 8

[1] Ia sedang memikirkan soal itu. [2] Tuan Lim akan terbang ke Bangkok bulan depan. [3] Tamu kami masih bercakap dengan ayah saya. [4] Ia telah berdoa. [5] Kamu tidak menutup pintu kemarin malam. [6] Kucing itu lagi berbaring di bawah méja. [7] Ia meninggal dunia dua minggu yang lalu. [8] Siapa mengendarakan mobil itu? [9] Saya akan memikirkan tentang itu. [10] Ia melihat temannya kemarin dahulu. [11] Ia tidak mengertinya. [12] Kita menggigit dengan gigi kita. [13] Meréka sekarang sedang berjalan di bawah pohon itu. [14] Kami kawin dua tahun yang lalu. [15] Saya duduk di dalam mobil tadi pagi. [16] Sékretaris saya mau pulang tiga bulan lagi. [17] Pada suatu hari sopir kami jatuh dari tangga. [18] Saya akan menyelesaikan pekerjaan itu bulan depan.

Exercise 10

[1] *bergigi*, Grandmother has no teeth. [2] *bermobil*, We went by car to Padang. [3] *bertepuktangan*, The audience clapped boisterously. [4] *berjanji*, He promised not to repeat that cruelty. [5] *berpakaian*, That girl likes to dress in blue. [6] *bertukar*, Didi and I have changed places. [7] *bertelur*, This hen has not laid an egg today. [8] *berciuman*, The two women kissed (each other). [9] *bertanam*, The villagers plant corn. [10] *berdarah*, Her wound is

bleeding. [11] *berempat*, There were four robbers. [12] *berselisih*, Why do you often quarrel?

Exercise 11

[1] *membaca*, Father is reading the newspaper. [2] *menggergaji*, It is not easy to saw this big beam. [3] *mendengar, menderu*, We heard the wind howling through the trees in the forest. [4] *menulis*, Poppi wrote a letter to her aunt. [5] *membunuh*, Somebody has killed the mad dog. [6] *mengapur*, The whitewasher is whitewashing the dirty wall. [7] *mendarat*, Our aeroplane landed safely at Karachi. [8] *menyimpan*, You must keep your money in the drawer. [9] *merokok*, He sat under the tree, smoking a cigarette. [10] *menyanyi, menari*, They sang and danced at the party. [11] *mencuci*, The servant did not do the laundry (wash the clothes) yesterday. [12] *menghitam*, The sky is getting dark; it will soon start raining. [13] *menyeberang*, Let us cross over. [14] *menjawab*, She did not want to answer the question.

Exercise 12

[1] melémpari, [2] memainkan, [3] menemukan, [4] mendengarkan, [5] meniduri, [6] menghamburkan, [7] menguliti, [8] melémparkan, [9] mengepalai, [10] menjualkan, [11] menempati, [12] meminjamkan, [13] merindukan, [14] menandatangani.

Exercise 13

[1] menggembirakan, [2] menyerang, [3] membandingkan, [4] mengisap, [5] beristirahat, mengalami, [6] meletakkan, [7] berhenti, beristirahat, [8] memperkokoh, [9] memperbudak, [10] memasuki, [11] berumur, [12] mengalir, [13] mengeringkan, bersinar, [14] menerima, [15] bersekolah, [16] menggarami, [17] memberikan, [18] bermain, [19] memanggil, [20] memukul.

Exercise 14

[1] Lagu merdu dinyanyikan oléhnya. [2] Usul Pak Diro meréka terima. [3] Keberaniannya dipuji orang. [4] Orang miskin itu akan kami tolong. [5] Perkara itu telah diselidiki oléh polisi. [6] Obéng saya belum dikembalikannya. [7] Buku itu kauterbitkan. [8] Rumah untuk anak-anak piatu itu didirikan oléhnya, *or*

Anak-anak piatu itu didirikan rumah oléhnya. [9] Belanja saya saya perkecil. [10] Hadiah itu kami sembunyikan di bawah lemari. [11] Jam 4 soré peluit paberik dibunyikan. [12] Gedung bioskop yang baru itu dibanjiri penonton. [13] Tas nyonya saya lihat di méja itu tadi. [14] Pedagang itu telah ditipu orang.

Exercise 15

[1] Tangis anak ini amat keras. Anak ini tangisnya amat keras. [2] Bunyi meriam itu dahsyat. Meriam itu bunyinya dahsyat. [3] Jawabnya dengan senyum. [4] Nyanyi kakak Mira amat merdu. Kakak Mira nyanyinya amat merdu. [5] Umur saya sekarang 40 tahun. [6] Panjang jembatan ini 200 méter. Jembatan ini panjangnya 200 méter. [7] Berat beras sekarung ini 50 kilogram. Beras sekarung ini beratnya 50 kilogram. [8] Kira meréka kita bersaudara. [9] Pikirnya soal itu dapat dipecahkan dengan gampang. [10] Tebal kulit ini 0·5 séntiméter. Kulit ini tebalnya 0·5 séntiméter. [11] Warna rambutnya coklat. Rambutnya warnanya (berwarna) coklat. [12] Gonggong anjing si Dodi keras sekali. Anjing si Dodi gonggongnya keras sekali. [13] Nyala lilin ini amat terang. Lilin ini nyalanya amat terang. [14] Luas taman ini 100 héktar. Taman ini luasnya 100 héktar.

Exercise 16

Ketua; perkumpulan; pertemuan; gunawan; pembantu; perkumpulan; halangan; rintangan; kemajuan. Pertemuan; tarian; nyanyian. Hidangan; minuman. Usahawan; pelukis; penari, peragawati; pertemuan; hartawan; perhiasan. Kelancaran; pertemuan; penyelenggaraan; ketua; karyawan. Penutupan; pertemuan; nyanyian.

The chairman of the 'Servias' association made a speech at the meeting. He said that there were many worthy citizens among the members of 'Servias', who had become active helpers in advancing the association. He hoped that there might not be any hindrances or obstacles which might hamper the progress of 'Servias'.

The meeting was enlivened by dances and songs, which were quite attractive. Refreshments and drinks were served to the guests. Business executives, artists, dancers and mannequins were present at the meeting.

The wives of the wealthy men wore sparkling ornaments. The smoothness of the meeting was due to the fact that arrangements were in the hands of the chairman himself, a veteran organizer. The meeting closed on a lively note with the singing of a song in which everybody joined.

Exercise 18a

[1] tak berawan, [2] jernih, bulat [3] ganjil [4] gemuk, [5] rindang, [6] sengit, banyak, terluka, [7] kehausan, [8] ramah, [9] bagus, [10] bambu, kuat, [11] cepat, [12] malas, marah, [13] terkunci, [14] kaya, kikir.

Exercise 18b

[1] sedih, buruk, [2] dalam, [3] hémat [4] longgar [5] bodoh, [6] terberat, [7] sederhana, [8] tajam, [9] halus, [10] terbangun, [11] dekat, banyak, [12] sukar *or* sulit, [13] sepi *or* sunyi, [14] rajin.

Exercise 19

[1] murah-murah. [2] anak-anak, bermain-main, [3] tawanan-tawanan, [4] seerat-eratnya, [5] serdadu-serdaduan, [6] kemérah-mérahan, [7] sejauh-jauhnya, [8] bercakap-cakap, [9] menjerit-jerit, orang-orang, [10] jelék-jelék, melihat-lihat, [11] bertahun-tahun, [12] berpeluk-pelukan, [13] dirobék-robék, [14] kucing-kucingan, [15] penumpang-penumpang, [16] mencari-cari.

Exercise 20

[1] papantulis, [2] lalulintas, [3] kaya-miskin, baik-hati, [4] cantik-juita, muda-belia, [5] menaruh hati, [6] membalas dendam, [7] ibukota, [8] hari-libur, [9] pasar-malam, [10] duta-besar, surat kepercayaan, [11] rumahmakan, [12] membanting-tulang, [13] angkatan udara, [14] mengucapkan selamat, perlombaan-lari, [15] pulang-pergi, [16] besarkepala.

Exercise 21

[1] Adik saya sering menonton film dengan teman-temannya, *or* Sering adik saya menonton film dengan teman-temannya. [2]

Nyonya Burns biasanya pergi berbelanja tiap-tiap pagi. *or* Biasanya Nyonya Burns pergi berbelanja tiap-tiap pagi. [3] Kamu
pernah tinggal di désa? *or* Pernahkah kamu tinggal di désa? [4]
Saya selalu membaca suratkabar setelah makan-malam, *or* Selalu
saya membaca suratkabar setelah makan-malam. [5] Meréka
hampir-hampir tidak percaya bahwa saya mendapat hadiah
pertama dalam kontés-nyanyi itu, *or* (*note: the separation of* 'hampir-
hampir' *and* 'tidak') Hampir-hampir meréka tidak percaya bahwa
saya mendapat hadiah pertama dalam kontés-nyanyi itu. [6] Kami
sekeluarga kadang-kadang pergi berpik-nik di tepi danau Toba,
or Kadang-kadang kami sekeluarga pergi berpik-nik di tepi danau
Toba. [7] Guru kami baru kembali dari luar negeri. [8] Ia tamat
sekolah menengah atas bulan yang lalu, *or* Bulan yang lalu ia
tamat sekolah menengah atas. [9] Perempuan itu mengatakannya
dengan sedih, *or* Dengan sedih perempuan itu mengatakannya.
[10] Anakmu yang bungsu sangat nakal, *or* Anakmu yang bungsu
nakal sangat. [11] Siapa yang tak pernah memberi sedekah kepada
pengemis itu? [12] Ia memainkan biola dengan sempurna, *or*
Dengan sempurna ia memainkan biola.

Exercise 22

A. enam, sepuluh, delapan, tiga, sembilan, tujuh, dua, satu,
lima, empat, sebelas, delapanbelas, enambelas, tigabelas, sembilanbelas, duabelas, tujuhbelas, empatbelas, limabelas, duapuluh,
duapuluh sembilan, empatpuluh delapan, tujuhpuluh satu, limapuluh, tigapuluh enam, enampuluh sembilan, delapanpuluh dua,
sembilanpuluh empat, dua ratus tiga, delapan ratus tujuhpuluh
dua, empat ratus tigapuluh enam, tujuh ratus delapanpuluh satu,
lima ratus sembilanpuluh empat, tujuh ribu tujuh ratus empatpuluh lima, delapanpuluh tujuh ribu empatpuluh lima, sembilan
ratus duabelas ribu delapan ratus tujuhpuluh lima, duajuta
empatpuluh lima ribu tujuh ratus tujuhpuluh enam.

B. empat seperempat, limapuluh tujuh setengah, enam ratus
delapan tigaperdelapan, tujuhratus limapuluh dua sebelas
perdelapanpuluh.

C. empat ditambah tujuh sama dengan sebelas, duabelas
ditambah sembilanbelas sama dengan tigapuluh satu.
delapan dikurangi dua sama dengan enam, seratus empat

dikurangi duapuluh delapan sama dengan tujuhpuluh enam.
sepuluh dikalikan tiga sama dengan tigapuluh, sembilanpuluh
dua dikalikan dua sama dengan seratus delapanpuluh empat.

tujuhpuluh dua dibagi delapan sama dengan sembilan, empat
ratus lima dibagi lima sama dengan delapanpuluh satu.

D. sebelas rupiah, tujuhpuluh empat rupiah, seratus tujuh
rupiah duapuluh lima sén.

E. jam tujuh pagi, jam delapan lebih seperempat malam, jam
sebelas kurang seperempat siang, jam empat kurang tiga menit
soré, jam setengah sepuluh pagi, jam duabelas siang, jam empat
lebih duapuluh lima menit soré; jam enam petang.

Exercise 23

[1] This river is 2 km long and 50 m wide. [2] Don't act high-
handedly when you are at some one's house. [3] The theatre
'Jutari' has 2000 seats; it is the biggest building in the town of P.
[4] 'Use your time well (as well as possible),' was the advice I often
got from my father. [5] The three murderers were sentenced to
death. [6] Tens of thousands of food packages were distributed
among the refugees. [7] Half the forest was burned up. [8] They
marched in threes when they entered the field. [9] Firstly, I want
to congratulate Kasino who won the first prize. [10] The whole
town was beflagged to celebrate the victory. [11] Both brothers
were kept in custody because they had committed forgery. [12]
Mr. Smith has shot three tigers.

Exercise 24a

[1] yang, [2] yang, [3] yang, [4] yang, [5] tempat, [6] barangsiapa, [7] yang, [8] apa, [9] yang, [10] tempat, [11] yang, [12]
siapa.

Exercise 24b

[1] Pangéran Diponegoro, yang mangkat pada tahun 1855,
   adalah pahlawan yang gagah-berani.
[2] Bunga mati yang kautempatkan di kamar saya seminggu
   yang lalu itu berbau busuk.
[3] Saya berjumpa dengan temanmu yang kauperkenalkan pada
   saya di pésta ulang-tahun si Sien.

[4] Singa, yang hidup di benua Afrika, adalah binatang yang kuat.

[5] Bekas guru saya, yang puteranya téwas dalam peperangan, baru mengunjungi saya.

[6] Kursi tempat saya duduk ini penuh dengan kutu busuk, *or* Kursi yang saja duduki ini penuh dengan kutu busuk.

[7] Sungai Musi, yang mengalir di Sumatera, adalah sungai yang dapat dilayari kapal-kapal besar. *or* Sungai Musi, yang dapat dilayari kapal-kapal besar, mengalir di Sumatera.

[8] Pulau Bali, yang terletak di sebelah timur Pulau Jawa, adalah pulau yang indah.

[9] Cendawan yang kaupegang tadi itu beracun.

[10] Orang dengan siapa kamu baru bercakap-cakap itu adalah kakak saya.

Exercise 26

[1] Saya telah menerima surat Tuan tertanggal 15 Juli. [2] Meréka akan berangkat ke London pada permulaan bulan Januari. [3] Sampaikın salamku kepada ibumu. [4] Kamu menaruh minat akan dékorasi rumah? [5] Jack bermain badminton tiap Sabtu soré. [6] Dapatkah Tuan mengabarkan kepada saya apakah Tuan mempunyai persediaan kertas sampul? [7] Tono lulus ujiannya Selasa yang lalu. [8] Kapankah bahan itu akan dikirim? [9] Toko buku itu mempunyai banyak langganan. [10] Saya akan mendapat libur pada pertengahan bulan Juni. [11] Mengapa kamu tak menjawab suratku? [12] Ayah saya akan pulang dalam bulan Maret.

Exercise 27

[1] ke, [2] di, [3] tentang, [4] di, hingga, [5] sepanjang, [6] tanpa (ke) pada, [7] untuk, [8] pada, [9] selama, [10] menuju ke, [11] sejak, [12] menjelang, [13] oléh, [14] di antara, [15] pada, kecuali, [16] karena, [17] dari, [18] dengan, [19] dari, [20] melalui.

Exercise 28

[1] Meskipun anak itu berusaha, ia tiada berhasil.

[2] Meskipun hujan, kami berjalan terus.

[3] Walaupan si Kadir dilarang pergi, ia pergi juga.

[4] Walaupun ia kaya, ia tidak sombong.

[5] Meréka berkata itu, seolah-olah meréka mengalami sendiri kejadian itu.

[6] Ia memakai perkakas saya, seolah-olah punyanya sendiri saja.

[7] Kami diperintahnya, seakan-akan kami pelayannya.

[8] Perempuan itu bertindak, seakan-akan ia yang berkuasa di rumah itu.

[9] Kamu boléh bermain-main di sini, asalkan tidak merusak halamanku.

[10] Pak Hasan minum obat, agar supaya sembuh dari penyakit-nya.

[11] Ia sedih, sebab sepédanya dicuri orang kemarin malam.

[12] Si Murti mengira bahwa Ali dan saya bersaudara.

Exercise 29

Policeman: 'Hey there, swimming in the river is not allowed.'
Man in the water: 'I'm not swimming, I'm drowning.'

Two deaf men met with each other in the street.
Amat: 'Hey Min, are you going out fishing?'
Amin: 'No, I'm going out fishing.'
Amat: 'Oh, I thought you were going out fishing.'

'Here are your sleeping-pills madam. Sufficient for three weeks.'
'Heavens! I don't want to sleep as long as that!'

The teacher was turning round the globe which lay on his table,
   then asked his pupils why the earth was flattened on both poles.
Parto, who thought that the teacher was staring at him, said:
   'Really it wasn't I who did it Sir, it was like that yesterday!'

A traveller saw his dog lying on the threshold.
'Come on, you, lazy dog,' he said, 'let's get going now.'
'Ah, I prefer to sleep,' the dog replied.

Exercise 30

[1] Ia berkata bahwa lampu-sepédanya dicuri orang.
[2] Saya bertanya kepada Kusin bagaimanakah dengan keséhatannya.
[3] Si Jayus berkata bahwa meréka tidak mau menunggu terlalu lama.
[4] Pak Karto bertanya kepadaku apa yang kupegang ini.
[5] Ia berkata kepadaku bahwa ia tidak kenal padamu.
[6] Ia menyuruh pengemis itu pergi.
[7] Ia mempersilakan kami duduk.
[8] Kamu mengatakan bahwa kamu telah selesai dengan pekerjaanmu.
[9] Si Polan ingin tahu siapa gadis itu.
[10] Ia melarang aku keluar.
[11] Saya menjawab bahwa bukan saya yang melakukan itu.
[12] Pak Guru bertanya apakah ada pertanyaan.

Exercise 32

[1] Tujuh (orang).
[2] Meréka melalaikan pekerjaan meréka, karena meréka sering berkelahi.
[3] Orang-orang jahat di dusun itu mengharapkan bagian warisan anak-anak laki-laki itu setelah kematian ayah meréka.
[4] Ia akan memperingatkan meréka terhadap orang-orang jahat itu.
[5] Ikatan tongkat-tongkat. Dan ia memerintahkan putera-puteranya untuk mematahkan ikatan itu.
[6] Tak seorangpun.
[7] Ia melepaskan tongkat-tongkat itu dari ikatannya dan mematahkannya satu demi satu.
[8] Meréka berseru bahwa kalau begitu seorang anakpun dapat melakukannya.
[9] Ia membandingkannya dengan persatuan putera-puteranya.
[10] Bila meréka bercerai meréka akan mudah menjadi mangsa musuh-musuh meréka.

VOCABULARY INDONESIAN-ENGLISH

abad century
 berabad-abad for ages
 pada abad keduapuluh
 in the twentieth century
abadi eternal
abai ... mengabaikan to
 underestimate, to neglect
abjad alphabet
abu ash
adab ... beradab polite,
 well-mannered
 peradaban civilization
adat customs
 adat-istiadat customs
adil just, fair
 keadilan justice
administrasi administration
adperténsi advertisement
agak somewhat, rather
agama religion
agén agent
agung distinguished
 tamu agung distinguished
 guest
ahli expert (noun)
air water
 air-mata tears
 mata-air spring
 air-bah flood
 air-terjun cataract,
 waterfall
ajak ... mengajak to invite
 ajakan invitation

ajar ... mengajar to teach
 mempelajari to study, to
 practise
 belajar to learn
 pelajar student
 pelajaran lesson
 pengajar teacher
 kurangajar imprudent
akal mind, intelligence,
 brains
 mengakali to cheat
akar root
akhir end (noun)
 berakhir to end
 akhirnya finally
akibat result, consequence
aktif active
aku I
 mengaku to confess
 pengakuan confession
alam nature
 ilmu alam physics
alat tool, implement,
 instrument
alir ... mengalir to stream,
 to flow
alis eyebrows
Allah God
amal charity, social work
aman safe
 keamanan safety
ambil ... mengambil to
 fetch, to bring

amplop envelope
ampun forgiveness
  mengampuni to forgive
anggrék orchid
angin wind, air
  masuk angin to catch a
  cold
angkat ... mengangkat to
carry, to lift, to take away
  anak angkat adopted
  child
angkut ... mengangkut to
transport
aniaya ... menganiaya to
torture
  penganiayaan torture
anjur ... menganjurkan to
recommend
antar ... mengantar to
accompany, to take, to
bring
antuk ... mengantuk
sleepy
antri (to) queue
apa what
  tidak apa apa never
  mind, it is all right
api fire
  keréta-api train
  gunung-api volcano
arah direction
arang charcoal
aruh ... mempengaruhi
to influence
  pengaruh influence
  terpengaruh to be
  influenced
  berpengaruh influential
arti meaning

berarti to mean
tiada berarti
  meaningless
arca statue
asal resources
asap smoke (noun)
asin salty
asing strange
  orang asing foreigner
aso ... mengaso to take a
rest
asrama boarding-house,
boarding school
atap roof
acara programme
atur ... mengatur to
arrange
  peraturan regulation
awan cloud
awas beware, take care
  awas anjing beware of the
  dog
ayam chicken, pullet, fowl
  anak ayam newly-
  hatched chicken
babi pig
  babi-hutan boar
badai storm
badan body
bajak plough
  membajak to plough
bajing squirrel
badut clown
bagai sort, similar to
  sebagai as
bagi ... membagi to divide
  bagian portion, section,
  department
  pembagian division

bahaya danger
  berbahaya dangerous,
    unsafe
bahkan even (adv.)
bahu shoulder
bayar ... membayar to
    pay
  bayaran payment
  pembayaran payment
  bayarkan to cause
    payment to be paid
bayi baby
bakar ... membakar to
    burn
  terbakar burned up
  kebakaran on fire
balas ... membalas to
    reply, to take revenge
    on
  pembalasan revenge
balik opposite, back
  berbalik to turn around
  membalikkan to turn
    (something) over
  sebaliknya on the
    contrary
  terbalik upside down
bangga proud
  membanggakan to be
    proud of
  kebanggaan pride
bangkit to rise, to get up
    (from a sitting position)
  membangkitkan to stir
    up, to cause
bangun to wake, to rise
    (from a lying position)
  membangunkan to raise,
    to erect

membanguni to awaken
    somebody
  bangunan building
  pembangunan building
    up
bangsa nation
  kebangsaan nationality
  lagu kebangsaan
    national anthem
banyak many, much
  banyak orang many
    people
  orang banyak the
    multitude, the masses
  memperbanyak to
    increase
  kebanyakan mostly, on
    the whole, generally
bantah ... membantah to
    answer back, to contradict
  berbantah to quarrel, to
    argue
  bantahan contradiction,
    argument
bantal pillow
banting ... membanting
    to throw down, to smash
  membanting-tulang to
    toil
bantu ... membantu to
    help, to co-operate
  bantuan assistance, aid
  pembantu assistant,
    co-worker
barat west
  barat-daya south-west
  barat-laut north-west
baring ... berbaring to lie,
    to recline

baris row, rank, line
  berbaris to range, to
    draw up
  barisan line, civic guard
basah wet
  'membasahkan to wet
  membasahi to moisten
batal void, invalid
  membatalkan to
    invalidate, to annul
  pembatalan annulment
batu stone
batuk, berbatuk cough, to
  cough
bawang onion
bébas free, at liberty
bécak trishaw
begini so, like this
begitu so, like that
bekas ex-, trace, track
  bekas murid ex-student
belah . . . membelah to split
  sebelah kiri left side
  sebelah kanan right side
  kedua belah both sides
bélok . . . membélok to
  turn (to the right or left)
benang thread
benda thing, object
  harta-benda goods,
    possessions
béngkok crooked, bent
  membéngkok to bend
beras rice
berat heavy
  memberatkan to burden,
    to make heavier
  keberatan to raise
    objections

berenang to swim
beri . . . memberi to give
  memberi-tahu to
    announce
  pemberitahuan
    announcement
  pemberian gift
bersih clean
  membersihkan to clean
  kebersihan neatness
biar let it be, so that
  membiarkan to leave
    (someone) alone, to
    tolerate
biasa common, accustomed,
  customary
  luar biasa extraordinary
  membiasakan diri to
    accustom oneself
biasanya usually
  kebiasaan habit
bibir lip
bingung confused
  membingungkan
    confusing
biru blue
bisik . . . berbisik-bisik to
  whisper
  membisikkan to whisper
    something
  membisiki to whisper
    something to someone
  bisikan whisper (noun)
bisu dumb
buang . . . membuang to
  throw away, to throw
  out
bujuk . . . membujuk to
  persuade

bukti proof
  membuktikan to prove
  terbukti evident
bumi earth, district
bungkus . . . membungkus
  to wrap
  bungkusan package,
  parcel
bunyi sound, noise
buruk bad, rotten
  memburuk to go bad, to
  rot
bongkar . . . membongkar
  to unpack, to break-up
boros extravagant
bosan to be bored
bocor to leak
botol bottle
campur mixed
  bercampur gaul dengan
  to associate with
  mencampuri to mix
  campuran mixture
cangkir cup
cara way, manner
coba . . . mencoba to try
contoh model
dada breast
daftar list
daging meat
dakwa . . . mendakwa to
  accuse
damai peace
derajat grade, degree, rank
debu dust
demam fever
derita . . . menderita to
  suffer
  tak terderita unbearable

derma alms
desak . . . mendesak to
  push
déwasa of age
  orang déwasa adult
  déwasa ini nowadays, at
  present
didik . . . mendidik to
  educate
doa prayer
domba sheep
duri thorn
dusta lie, falsehood
  mendusta to lie (to tell a
  falsehood)
dorong . . . mendorong to
  push
dosin dozen
émbér pail, bucket
embus . . . mengembus to
  blow
empuk soft, tender
entah I don't know
énténg light, not heavy
éncok rheumatism
erat tight (adj.)
és ice
faham conception
  salah faham
  misunderstanding
fakultas faculty
fihak side, faction
  berfihak to belong to the
  faction of
gagah strong, robust
gagal to fail
gajah elephant
gaji salary
gali . . . menggali to dig

gambar drawing, painting
  menggambar to draw, to sketch
ganggu . . . mengganggu to disturb
ganti . . . mengganti to change
gantung . . . menggantung to hang
garam salt
garuk . . . menggaruk to scratch
gatal itch
gelang bracelet
gelap dark
gemar akan fond of
gembira happy, gay
gemuk thick-set, stout, fat
géndong . . . menggéndong to carry on the back
giat diligent
gila mad
girang pleased, delighted
goda . . . menggoda to tease
gula sugar
guna use (noun)
  berguna useful
  menggunakan to use
goyang . . . menggoyang to shake
goréng . . . menggoréng to fry
gosok . . . menggosok to rub
habis out of stock, done, finished
hakim judge
halaman yard, garden, pag of a book

halus fine, soft, tender, delicate, refined
hampir nearly
hapus . . . menghapus to rub out, to erase
hasil yield, produce, result
  menghasilkan to yield, to produce, to result
hati liver, mind, heart
hawa weather, atmosphere
hémat economical
héran surprised
hidung nose
hitung . . . menghitung to count, to calculate
hubung . . . menghubungkan to connect
huruf letter
hotél hotel
hukum law
hukuman punishment
  menghukum to punish, to sentence
ikan fish
ikat bundle, sheaf
  mengikat to tie
iklim climate
ikut . . . mengikut to follow to join
inap . . . menginap stay (overnight or longer)
injak . . . menginjak to tread
iris . . . mengiris to slice
isap . . . mengisap to suck
isi contents
  berisi to contain
jaga . . . menjaga to guard, to watch
jahat bad, criminal (adj.)

penjahat   criminal (noun)
jahit . . . menjahit   to sew
   penjahit   tailor
jalan   street, way
   berjalan   to walk
jam   hour, watch
janggut   beard
jantung   heart
jari   finger
jarum   needle
jelek   ugly
jemput . . . menjemput   to
   call for
jempol   thumb, excellent
jengkel   to be annoyed
jeruk   lemon or orange
   (citrus fruit)
jijik   nasty
jiwa   soul
jujur   honest
jumlah   sum
kagum   amazed
kayu   wood
kaki   foot, leg
kakus   toilet, W.C.
kambing   goat
kampung   village, quarter
kanan   right (hand)
kancing   button
kantong   sack, bag
kaus   socks (knitted material)
   baju kaus   singlet
kapas   cotton-wool (for
   medical purposes)
kapok   kapok
karang . . . mengarang   to
   compose
   karangan   composition
karcis   ticket

kacang   bean, peanut
kejam   cruel
kelapa   coconut
keliling   round
ke mari   hither, this way
kena   hit, struck,
   contaminated
kendaraan   vehicle
   mengendarai   to ride, to
   drive
kentang   potato
kentara   obvious
kerbau   buffalo
kering   dry (adj.)
   mengeringkan   to dry
keringat   perspiration
   berkeringat   to perspire
kecéwa   disappointed
kecuali   except
khayal   imagination,
   hallucination, fantasy
khas   typical
khusus   particular
   pada khususnya
   particularly
khotbah   sermon
kiri   left (hand)
kodok   frog
kompor   stove
kursi   chair
kulit   hide, skin, leather
kumis   moustache
kuning   yellow
kurban or korban   victim
kurus   thin (of persons)
lahir   born
   kelahiran   birth
laku   much sought after, sold,
   valid

lalai indifferent, thoughtless
  melalaikan to neglect
lamar ... melamar to
  apply
  pelamar applicant
lambat slow
lampu lamp
langganan customer
léhér neck
lekas quick
lelah tired
lemah weak
lémpar ... melémpar to
  throw
lengan arm
lengkap complete
lepas loose, free, fled
  melepaskan to let loose,
    to let go, to untie, to
    detach
lidah tongue
lipat ... melipat to fold
listrik electricity
luas wide, outstretched
lubang hole
  melubangi to make a hole
lukis ... melukis to paint,
  to draw
  lukisan painting, drawing
  pelukis painter, artist
lutut knee
  berlutut to kneel
loncat ... meloncat to
  jump
mabok drunk, intoxicated
macam sort, kind
majalah magazine
maju to go forward, to
  advance

kemajuan progress
maksud aim, intention
  bermaksud untuk to
    have the intention of
malu shy, ashamed,
  shamefaced
manis sweet
manusia human being
matahari sun
mémang by nature,
  self-evident, indeed
mendung cloudy
mentimun cucumber
mesjid or **masjid** mosque
mimpi or **impian** dream
  (noun)
  bermimpi to dream
minyak oil
  minyak-kacang salad-oil
  minyak-kelapa coconut-
    oil
  minyak-tanah kerosene
muat ... memuat to
  contain, to comprise
  memuati to load
  muatan cargo
muka face
mulut mouth
mundur to go backward, to
  retreat
musim season
  musim hujan rainy
    season
  musim kemarau dry
    season
nafas breath
  bernafas to breathe
naik to climb, to ascend
nakal naughty

nanti later (indication of future time)
  menanti to wait
nasihat or **naséhat** advice
  menasihatkan to advise
  penasihat adviser
natal . . . Hari Natal Christmas
nénék grandmother
  nénék-moyang ancestors
ngawur tosh, foolish talk
nomor number
nyata clear, obvious
  menyatakan to make clear
nyawa soul
obat medicine
ombak wave (noun)
omél . . . mengomél to grumble
olok-olok ridicule (noun)
  mengolok-olok to ridicule
ongkos cost, total
opsir officer
otak brain
pahit bitter
pajak tax
paku nail
  memaku to nail
paksa . . . memaksa to force, to compel
  keadaan terpaksa (state of) emergency
  terpaksa forced, compelled, not free, constrained
panggang . . . memanggang to roast

pangkat rank
payah difficult, exhausted
  sakit payah mortally ill
payung umbrella
pecah broken
  memecahkan to break, to smash
pegawai official, employer
pelihara . . . memelihara to rear, to breed, to keep, to maintain
pemandangan panorama
penyakit disease
penting important
periksa . . . memeriksa to examine, to look into, to investigate
perut stomach
pesan errand
pidato speech, lecture
pipa pipe
puas satisfied
putus cut off
  memutuskan to cut off, to break off, to decide
pompa . . . memompa pump, to pump
rambut hair
rencana programme
roboh to collapse
rumput grass
rupa form, appearance
  merupakan to have the appearance of
  menyerupai to resemble
  serupa similar
rombak . . . merombak to break up
rombongan group

sabun soap

sahut ... menyahut to reply, to retort

saksi witness

menyaksikan to witness

saku pocket

salin ... menyalin to copy

sama same, even

sama sekali altogether

sama juga all the same

menyamai to resemble

menyamakan to compare

sambung ... menyambung to connect

sangka ... menyangka to suppose, to suspect

sayap wing

sembahyang prayer

bersembahyang to pray

sementara meanwhile

senang pleased, delighted

séndok spoon

sépak ... menyépak to kick

sétan devil

setia loyal

sikat brush

menyikat to brush

siram ... menyiram to pour, to water

suara voice, sound

susu milk

sopan polite

taksir ... menaksir to value, to estimate

tali string, rope

tanda sign (noun)

tanda-mata token, gift

tanda-tangan signature

menandatangani to sign

tangga ladder, step

tanggung ... menanggung to guarantee

tanggung-jawab responsibility

tebal thick (of things)

telan ... menelan to swallow

telanjang nude

telinga ear

tengah middle

terang clear, bright

terus terang frank(ly)

menerangkan to explain

tinta ink

tiru ... meniru to imitate

toko shop

tulang bone

ubah ... berubah to change (intransitive)

mengubah to change (transitive)

uji ... menguji to examine, to test

ukur ... mengukur to measure

ukuran measurement

ulang ... mengulangi to repeat

berulang-ulang again and again

ulang-tahun birthday

ulung skilful, cunning

umum general, general public

pada umumnya generally

di muka umum in public

umpama example

umpamanya for example
upah payment
urat muscle
urung ... mengurungkan to cancel
urus ... mengurus to manage, to administer
   pengurus management, administration, manager

wakil representative
   mewakili to represent
wanita woman
warung small shop, small restaurant
yakin convinced
yatim orphan
y.b.l yang baru lalu last, recent

VOCABULARY ENGLISH–INDONESIAN

aback **mundur**
abandon **tinggalkan,
  meninggalkan**
abbreviate **singkat,
  menyingkat**
abbreviation **singkatan**
ability **kemahiran,
  kebisaan, kecakapan**
able **mahir, bisa, cakap**
abolish **hapuskan,
  menghapuskan**
about (more or less) **lebih
  kurang**
absent **absén**
accept **terima, menerima**
acceptance **penerimaan**
accident **kecelakaan**
accustomed **biasa**
ache **sakit**
acquaintance **kenalan**
add **tambah, menambah**
addition **tambahan**
adjourn **tunda, menunda**
adult **orang déwasa**
advertisement **adperténsi,
  iklan**
afoot **berjalan kaki**
afraid **takut**
again **lagi**
agree **setuju**
agreement **persetujuan**
aid (noun) **bantuan**
aim (noun) **tujuan**
air **hawa, udara**
airfield **lapangan-terbang**

allow **perboléhkan,
  memperboléhkan**
aloud **keras**
alter **(r)ubah, merubah**
alteration **perubahan**
amount **jumlah**
apologize **minta maaf**
ashamed **malu**
assemble **berkumpul**
assist **bantu, membantu**
assistant **pembantu**
astonish (transitive)
  menghérankan
astonished **héran**
attempt (verb) **coba,
  mencoba;**
  (noun) **percobaan**
attend **hadiri, menghadiri**
author **pengarang**
avoid **hindari,
  menghindari**
baby **bayi**
bag **tas**
banana **pisang**
bargain **tawar, menawar;**
  (noun) **tawaran**
basket **keranjang**
beach **pantai**
beautiful **indah, cantik**
beforehand **sebelumnya**
beggar **pengemis**
bench **bangku**
beware **awas**
bewildered **bingung**
big **besar**

bill **rékening**

bind **ikat, mengikat**

black **hitam**

blanket **selimut**

blue **biru**

boil **rebus, merebus**

bone **tulang**

boss **majikan**

bottle **botol**

bowl **mangkuk**

box **kotak**

brave **berani**

break (transitive) **pecahkan, memecahkan;** (intransitive) **pecah**

breakfast **makan-pagi, sarapan**

bridge **jembatan**

bring **bawa, membawa**

brother-in-law **ipar laki-laki**

brush (verb) **sikat, menyikat** (noun) **sikat**

buffalo **kerbau**

burn (transitive) **bakar, membakar** (intransitive) **menyala**

button **kancing**

call **panggil, memanggil**

call (for) **jemput, menjemput** (on) **singgah**

cancel **batalkan, membatalkan**

candidate **calon**

candle **lilin**

candy **manisan, permén**

carry **angkat, mengangkat**

case (box) **peti**

catch **tangkap, menangkap**

chance (noun) **kesempatan**

chaos **kekacauan**

chaotic **kacau**

chat (verb) **mengobrol** (noun) **obrolan**

chicken **ayam**

chocolate **coklat**

choice **pilihan**

choose **pilih, memilih**

church **geréja**

Christmas **Hari Natal**

cigarette **rokok**

cinema **bioskop**

class **kelas**

clean **bersih**

clear (of speech, etc.) **jelas** (of water, sky) **jernih**

clothing **pakaian**

coat **jas**

coconut **kelapa**

coffee **kopi**

collect **kumpulkan, mengumpulkan**

collection **kumpulan, koléksi**

collide **tubruk, menubruk**

collision **tubrukan**

comb (verb) **sisir, menyisir** (noun) **sisir**

commit **melakukan**

common **umum**

complete **lengkap**

composition (piece of writing) **karangan** (piece of music) **gubahan**

condition **keadaan**

confess **mengaku**
content **puas**
contribute **sumbang,
menyumbang**
contribution **sumbangan**
conversation **percakapan**
convey **sampaikan,
menyampaikan**
cool **sejuk**
correct **benar, betul**
cow **sapi**
crossing **persimpangan,
perempatan**
custom **adat, kebiasaan**
customer **langganan**
danger **bahaya**
dangerous **berbahaya**
dark **gelap**
deaf **tuli**
decide **putuskan,
memutuskan**
decision **keputusan**
deed **perbuatan**
depend (upon) **tergantung
(pada)**
desk **bangku-tulis**
develop **berkembang**
development
perkembangan
differ **berbéda**
difference **perbédaan**
dining-room **kamar-makan**
dinner **makan-malam**
direct **langsung**
dishonest **tak jujur**
dispensary **apotik**
disturb **ganggu,
mengganggu**
disturbance **gangguan**

divorce (verb, intransitive)
bercerai;
(transitive)
menceraikan
(noun) **perceraian**
draw (a figure, etc.) **gambar,
menggambar**
(a cart, etc.) **tarik,
menarik**
dream (verb) **bermimpi**
(noun) **impian**
dry (verb) **jemur,
menjemur**
(adj.) **kering**
duty **kewajiban**
early **pagi, pagi pagi**
edge **pinggir, tepi**
educate **didik, mendidik**
education **pendidikan**
e.g. (for instance) **misalnya,
umpamanya**
embassy **kedutaan**
employee **pegawai**
empty **kosong**
engine **mesin**
estimate **taksir, menaksir**
evidence **bukti**
evident **nyata**
examination **ujian**
examine **uji, menguji**
examiner **penguji**
except **kecuali**
exercise (verb) **melatih;**
(noun) **latihan**
exhibit **pamérkan,
memamérkan**
exhibition **paméran**
expect **harapkan,
mengharapkan**

expectation **pengharapan**

experience (verb) **alami, mengalami**

(noun) **pengalaman**

expert **ahli**

fact **kenyataan, fakta**

fail **gagal**

false **palsu**

family **keluarga, pamili**

fast (go without food) **berpuasa**

(rapid) **cepat**

fault **salah**

fear **takut**

fee **bayaran**

fence **pagar**

fertile **subur**

fill **isi, mengisi**

finger **jari**

finish **selesaikan, menyelesaikan, tamatkan menamatkan**

finished **selesai, tamat**

floor **lantai**

fly (verb) **terbang**

(insect) **lalat**

fold (verb) **lipat, melipat**

(noun) **lipatan**

follow **ikuti, mengikuti**

fool **gila**

furniture **prabot**

game **permainan**

garage **garasi**

garden **kebun**

gradual **lambat laun**

grass **rumput**

green **hijau**

grief **kesedihan**

grieve **sedih**

guilty **bersalah**

gun **bedil**

habit **kebiasaan**

hammer **palu**

headache **sakit kepala**

heal (intransitive) **sembuh**

(transitive) **menyembuhkan**

health **keséhatan**

healthy **séhat**

heat (verb) **panaskan, memanaskan**

(noun) **panas**

holiday **hari-libur**

history **sejarah**

hit **pukul, memukul**

hold **pegang, memegang**

horse **kuda**

hospitable **ramah-tamah**

host **tuan-rumah**

hostess **nyonya-rumah**

household **rumah-tangga**

hurt (verb) **lukai, melukai**

(pred. adj.) **terluka**

husband **suami**

ice **és**

idea **idé, pikiran**

illiterate **buta huruf**

imitate **tiru, meniru**

impatient **tak sabar**

import (verb) **mengimpor**

(noun) **impor**

important **penting**

impossible **tak mungkin**

impudent **kurangajar**

incident **kejadian**

income **penghasilan**

indeed **mémang**

influence (verb) **pengaruhi,
mempengaruhi;**
(noun) **pengaruh**
inform **kabarkan,
mengabarkan**
information **keterangan**
ink **tinta**
inquire **minta keterangan**
inspect **periksa, memeriksa**
intelligent **cerdik**
intend **bermaksud**
intention **maksud**
interest **perhatian**
interesting **menarik**
introduce **perkenalkan,
memperkenalkan**
invite **undang,
mengundang**
invitation **undangan**
iron (verb) **seterika,
menyeterika**
(tool) **seterika**
(metal) **besi**
island **pulau**
itch **gatal**
jam **selai**
jar **toplés**
jealous **iri**
job **pekerjaan**
join **ikut**
joke (verb) **bersenda-
gurau**
(noun) **sendagurau**
journey **perjalanan**
joyful **gembira**
judge **hakim**
juice **air perah**
jump **lompat, melompat**
kettle **kétél**

key **kunci**
kill **bunuh, membunuh**
kind (sort) **jenis, macam**
(hearted) **baik-(hati)**
kitchen **dapur**
knee **lutut**
kneel **berlutut**
knife **pisau**
knowledge **pengetahuan**
labourer **pekerja**
lack (of) **kekurangan**
ladder **tangga**
land **darat, negeri, tanah**
language **bahasa**
late (after appointed time)
terlambat
laundry (on the line)
jemuran
(works) **penatu**
lavatory **kakus, W.C.**
(pronounced: **wé sé**)
law **hukum**
lazy **malas**
leak **bocor**
leather **kulit**
lecture **kuliah**
lecturer **dosén**
leisure **waktu senggang**
lemon **jeruk**
lemonade **limun**
letter **surat**
lie (of people) **berbaring**
(of things) **terletak**
(untruth) **dusta**
lip **bibir**
list **daftar**
livelihood **nafkah**
liver **hati**
loaf **roti**

lobster **kepiting**
looker-on **penonton**
louse **kutu**
lovely **cantik, indah**
low **rendah**
luck **untung**
lucky **beruntung**
lunch **makan-siang**
luxurious **méwah**
luxury **keméwahan**
machine **mesin**
mackintosh **jas-hujan**
maid-servant **babu, pelayan**
mainly **terutama**
manner **aturan, cara**
man-servant **jongos,
pelayan**
mark (sign) **tanda**
(cypher) **nilai, angka**
market **pasar**
marriage **pernikahan,
perkawinan**
marry **menikah, kawin**
massage **urut**
match (game) **pertandingan**
(safety match) **korék**
mattress **tikar**
meal **makan**
meaning **arti, maksud**
medicine **obat**
mend **betulkan,
membetulkan**
middle **tengah**
middle-sized **ukuran sedang**
milk **susu**
mind **ingat**
mistake **kesalahan**
misunderstand **salah
mengerti**

mix **campur**
mixture **campuran**
money **uang**
monsoon **musim**
wet monsoon **musim
hujan**
dry monsoon **musim
kemarau**
monument **tugu**
Moslem **orang Islam**
mosque **mesjid** or
masjid
mosquito **nyamuk**
motor **motor**
mouse **tikus**
mouth **mulut**
mud **lumpur**
nail (of iron) **paku**
(of the finger) **kuku**
napkin **serbét**
narrow **sempit**
nationality **kebangsaan**
naturally **tentu saja**
neat **bersih**
necessary **perlu**
neck **léhér**
need (verb) **perlu**
(noun) **keperluan**
needless **percuma**
new year **tahun baru**
nice **baik, bagus**
nonsense **omong kosong**
nose **hidung**
nowadays **déwasa ini,
sekarang**
nurse **jururawat**
oblige **terpaksa**
occur **terjadi**
odd **anéh, ganjil**

offer (verb) **tawarkan, menawarkan**
(noun) **tawaran**
omit **hapuskan, menghapuskan**
onion **bawang**
opinion **pendapat**
orchid **anggrék**
owe **berhutang**
owing (to) **disebabkan (oléh)**
owner **pemilik**
ox **lembu**
oyster **kerang**
packet **bungkusan**
page **halaman**
pain **sakit**
pale **pucat**
pan **kuali, panci**
panorama **pemandangan**
peel **kupas, mengupas**
pepper **merica**
perfect **sempurna**
perhaps **boléh jadi, mungkin**
perspire **berkeringat**
petrol **bénsin**
petroleum **minyak-tanah**
photographer **tukang-potrét**
pill **pil**
pillow **bantal**
pin **peniti**
pinch **cubit, mencubit**
pine-apple **nenas**
pity **kasihan**
plate **piring**
pocket **saku**
polite **sopan**

pork **daging babi**
postman **tukang-pos**
pour **tuang, menuang**
prefer **lebih suka**
prescription **resép**
primary school **sekolah dasar**
printing-office **percétakan**
profession **jabatan**
promise (verb) **berjanji**
(noun) **janji**
proof **bukti**
proposal **usul**
propose **usulkan, mengusulkan**
prove **buktikan, membuktikan**
pump **pompa**
puncture **bocor**
question **pertanyaan**
quick **cepat, lekas**
quiet **sepi, tenang**
quinine **kina**
rack **rak**
racket **rakét, réket**
rank **pangkat**
rare **jarang**
rather **agak**
raw **mentah**
reach **capai, mencapai**
ready **siap**
reason **sebab**
receive **terima, menerima**
refusal **penolakan**
refuse (verb) **menolak**
relative **sanak**
relatives **sanak-saudara**
religion **agama**
repeat **ulangi, mengulangi**

responsibility **tanggung-jawab**

responsible **bertanggung-jawab**

result (verb) **hasilkan, menghasilkan;** (noun) **hasil**

right (ant. of wrong) **benar** (ant. of left) **kiri**

rope **tampar**

round **bulat**

rub **gosok, menggosok**

sack **karung, sak**

sacred **suci**

salary **gaji**

sand **pasir**

sandal **sandal**

seat **tempat-duduk**

secondary school **sekolah menengah pertama**

sentence (of words) **kalimat** (at a trial) **hukuman**

show (verb) **pertunjukkan, mempertunjukkan** (noun) **pertunjukan**

simple **sederhana**

skin **kulit**

small **kecil**

soap **sabun**

soft **halus**

soon **segera**

sound **suara**

south **selatan**

speed **kecepatan**

spice **rempah**

spoon **séndok**

station **setasiun**

steal **curi, mencuri**

stone **batu**

story **cerita**

stove **kompor**

string **tali**

stroll **berjalan-jalan**

subscribe **berlangganan**

subscriber **langganan**

sugar **gula**

suit-case **kopor**

sweet **manis**

swim **berenang**

syrup **setrup**

table-cloth **taplak-méja**

tailor **penjahit**

tall **tinggi**

tariff **harga**

taste **rasa**

taxi **taksi**

tea **téh**

temple **kuil**

temporary **sementara**

test **tés**

thin (of people) **kurus** (of things) **tipis**

think **berpikir**

thread **benang**

through **melalui**

throughout **seluruh, sepanjang**

ticket **karcis**

tie (verb) **ikat, mengikat** (necktie) **dasi**

tobacco **tembakau**

tongs **tang**

tongue **lidah**

tool **alat, perkakas**

tooth-brush **sikat-gigi**

towel **handuk**

travel **bepergian**

trousers **celana**

try **coba, mencoba**
turn (verb) **bélok, membélok**
  (of a road, etc.) **bélokan**
  (in reading, etc.) **giliran**
typewriter **mesintik**
tyre **ban**
ugly **buruk, jelék**
umbrella **payung**
unbearable **tak tertahan**
uncertain **tak pasti**
understand **mengerti**
underwear **pakaian dalam**
uneven **ganjil**
uniform **seragam**
unknown **tak terkenal**
unless **kalau tidak, asal tidak, kecuali**
unpleasant **tak menyenangkan**
unreasonable **tak masuk akal**
untidy **kotor**
use (verb) **gunakan, menggunakan**
  (noun) **guna**
useful **berguna**
useless **tak berguna**
vacant **kosong**
vacation **liburan**
valley **lembah**
valuable **berharga, bernilai**
value **harga, nilai**
vase **tempat-bunga**
vehicle **kendaraan**
vendor **penjaja, orang jaja**
view **pemandangan**
vinegar **cuka**
visa **visa**

visit (verb) **kunjungi, mengunjungi**
  (noun) **kunjungan**
voice **suara**
volcano **gunung-api**
vomit **muntah**
vote (verb) **pungut suara, memungut suara**
  (noun) **pemungutan suara**

wage **gaji, salaris**
waist **pinggang**
wait **tunggu, menunggu**
waiter **pelayan réstoran**
waiting-room **kamar-tunggu**
wall **dinding**
wardrobe **lemari-pakaian**
wash-stand **waskom**
waste (of time) **buang waktu**
  (of money) **buang uang**
  (material) **sampah, kotoran**
water **air**
weak **lemah**
wear **pakai, memakai**
weather **hawa, udara**
weigh **timbang, menimbang**
weight **berat**
west **barat**
while **sambil, sementara**
whole **seluruh**
wind **angin**
wood **kayu**
world **dunia**
worry **kuatir**
wrist-watch **jam tangan**
X ray **sinar X**

yard **halaman**
yell **jerit, menjerit**
young **muda**
youth **anak muda, kaum muda**

zeal **semangat**
zealous **bersemangat**
zero **nol**
zinc **séng**
zoo **kebun-binatang**

SAMOAN

C. C. MARSACK

A practical introduction to the language of the Samoan islands, written both for the beginner and the student of Polynesian languages.

An account of the Samoan alphabet and pronunciation is followed by a series of carefully graded lessons covering different aspects of the language. Exercises and translations are included throughout the book which culminates in an extensive vocabulary list. A useful section on the socially important courtesy language is also included.

TEACH YOURSELF BOOKS

MODERN PERSIAN

JOHN MACE

This book provides a complete course in modern Persian, the national language of Iran, for the beginner and student alike.

The division of the book into three parts enables the student to progress smoothly from one stage of the language to another. The Persian script, grammar and vocabulary-building are each covered in a clear and concise manner and the exercises, complete with keys, at the end of each section, are invaluable in bringing the student to a sound working knowledge of the language. There is also an extensive bilingual vocabulary.

TEACH YOURSELF BOOKS

JAPANESE

C. J. DUNN AND S. YANADA

This book is designed to take the student with no previous experience of Japanese to the point where he is able to hold a conversation on many non-technical subjects with confidence. Principal points of grammar and a basic vocabulary are introduced in a series of graded lessons, and there are supplementary sections on the socially essential respect language and conversational usage. Romanised spelling is used throughout.

TEACH YOURSELF BOOKS